Mastering College

Darren Sapp

Copyright © 2019 by Darren Sapp
All rights reserved.

www.darrensapp.com

No part of this book may be reproduced in any form or by any electronic or mechanical means including information storage and retrieval systems, without permission in writing from the author. The only exception is by a reviewer, who may quote short excerpts in a review.

Collins & Halsey Publishers / May 2019

ISBN: 978-0-9989830-2-8

Cover Design: www.vividcovers.com
Formatting: www.polgarusstudio.com
Editing: www.pure-text.net

Also by Darren Sapp

FICTION
Fire on the Flight Deck
The Fisher Boy
Special Force: A World War II Commando Novel
Summer of '79

NON-FICTION
Aaron Bank and the Early Days of US Army Special Forces

Discover more at darrensapp.com
and join the mailing list.

*Dedicated to C.R. Self,
a teacher unlike any other.*

Contents

1. Why You Should Read This Book 1
2. Small Bites 7
3. Syllabus Shock 13
4. Testmaster Or Teacher's Pet 21
5. Read Faster While Retaining More 29
6. The No-Gimmick Way To Memorize 37
7. The Quick And Clean Guide To Writing Those Papers.......... 43
8. Synchronizing Mind And Body... 53
9. *A Beautiful Mind* Was Right About Teamwork 59
10. To Greek Or Not To Greek... 63
11. The Math Lab Is Your Friend 67
12. Sheep And Wolves 73
13. We're Hiring.. 81
14. Preparing To Launch 89

Acknowledgments 93
Bibliography And Suggested Resources 95

An investment in knowledge pays the best interest.
—Benjamin Franklin

1.

WHY YOU SHOULD READ THIS BOOK

"If you don't go to school, you'll be doing this when you're my age," Ronnie said.

My fifty-five-year-old fellow worker had just crawled through the manhole of a water tank he'd been sandblasting. I had just crawled out of another tank where the diameter was less than my height. The heat from a Texas afternoon in August baked the sand that crept its way inside my shirt and down my back. Sweat drenched my clothes. His words terrified me, and I filled out an application for college the next day.

I've always considered that work honorable. I applaud those who work with their hands. However, it wasn't for me. I wanted something different. I wanted to work in a field that required a college education. A boss of mine often says, "Get paid for what you know, not what you do." That statement captures what I felt at the time.

Do you know why you're going to college? To obtain a degree, no doubt, but what will that really do for you? I'm asking a deeper question. What value have you placed on that degree? Maybe you love working with numbers and see yourself as the chief financial officer for a large corporation. Perhaps the excitement of an emergency room is in your future. Don't think of that degree as merely a means to end. Find value in every single course. Strive to master each one because they all serve toward your well-rounded education—and, more, toward what that education will really do for you.

If you're unsure of your ultimate calling and are simply compelled to earn a bachelor's degree, know that this applies to you as well.

I've used some or all of every college course I've ever taken. And, yes, that includes algebra, philosophy, and French. Imagine yourself interviewing for that dream position, leading a team, or closing a business transaction. Know that those history courses will help you speak more intelligently about the world or that introduction to psychology gives you insight others don't have.

College builds your mind. The building blocks are those courses. Learn to find value in every block. This little book teaches you dozens and dozens of ways to make that easier, enjoyable, and more efficient. It's about working smarter, not harder. You might hear that phrase again.

Don't regret that literature course. Make it your mission to find ten things from it that you'll use in a later course or your future job. Embrace it. Students that understand why they're taking a course and are pursuing their degree achieve better grades, have better attitudes, and find college a more rewarding experience. If you're only there doing the "time," you'll find it harder to focus, study, and complete assignments.

Did I master college? Not at first. I struggled greatly with poor study habits, a negative attitude, and a muddled sense of direction. I spent many semesters with a mix of A's, B's, and C's. Just average. Somewhat below average. I did finish strong, though, receiving a 3.5 GPA in my last twelve courses. I later earned a 3.88 GPA in a thirty-hour seminary graduate program and then attended another school for a Master of Arts, finishing with a 3.97 GPA.

What changed? The following chapters will outline the practices and principles I used to master college. I learned what successful students around me were doing. I asked those scoring top grades and those affirming that they weren't stressed over school how they did it. None of the steps require savant-like gifts but rather a focused effort to succeed. Now that four of my five children are finishing or attending college, I've noticed their experiences and expectations are similar to the ones I had. Technology changes, but the methods to succeed have not. They're tried and true.

I'll share one with you now, and this practice might be the most important one of all. I realized that I never looked back and wished I'd watched more TV. I never looked back and felt satisfied with a "C" average. I never looked back and wished I had skipped a semester. I developed a habit of imaging how I'd feel at the end of the semester and used that to direct current behavior. Doing so, I did often look back with great joy that I set priorities and finished the semester strong. This type of thinking became a drug. That successful class built into a chain of semesters and then degrees.

Does your GPA matter? The short answer is yes. It matters while you're in college for departmental scholarships, organizations you may want to join, transfer options, and a host of other things. Your final GPA may determine graduate school acceptance or whether you qualify for a teacher certification program. Certain employers may make a hiring decision based on it. Imagine adding a 3.9 to your resume. You may not actually write it on there, but if a hiring manager notices your degree in architecture and asks how you did, there's nothing wrong with stating, "I did well and earned a 3.9 GPA."

This introduction is short and sweet. Why? Because I want you to embrace the mindset of absorbing information in small bites. I want you to understand the power of increments, which I'll explain in the next chapter. Most of the chapters are short as well. You can easily read this book in one sitting, but you might consider reading one chapter per day. One increment per day. One step per day. One bite per day. College is mastered in increments. One semester at a time. One class at a time. One project at a time. Focus on one thing, do it well, and move on.

Occasionally, I'll challenge you to think like a professor, roommate, or others. This is designed so you think beyond your own self-interest and gain an advantage by knowing the best way you can work with a partner. You should be looking for win-win relationships in everything you do. You'll find that some of the most successful business people always look for a way to help someone else, whether it be a customer, potential customer, employee, or associate.

I won't discuss SAT strategies, how to earn scholarships, or tips for getting accepted to your dream college. There are plenty of fine works on that as well as apps and websites.

I will emphasize that much of your success in college will be found on a campus where you're comfortable, the school is affordable, and there are plenty of resources to support your major. I'll teach you to drastically reduce test preparation time and write papers with less pain. My goal is to show you all those little things I wish I had known on day one.

This book is designed to be read prior to or during your senior year in high school. It's what I've been teaching my kids from junior high school work and as they prepare for college. Many of the concepts can be used during high school, and it's not too late to read this well into college. After all, I learned most of them late in my college career.

I'll use a word or two you may need to look up. I don't do that to wow you with my vocabulary, but rather to set you on the path of expanding your own. It's vital for reading, classroom note-taking, writing, testing, and conversation. If you run across a word and are not sure of the meaning, stop! Consider the context and try to understand it. If needed, do a quick search for the definition and then try to work that word into your day either through writing or conversation. We should use words that are easily understood by those we converse with or write for, but the goal of this book is to help you build skills to make college easier. Part of that means building your vocabulary.

Throughout this book, I'll mention or recommend other books and courses you might consider to strengthen your knowledge base.

Don't let this overwhelm you. Consider them optional reading for items that pique your interest. After all, this book isn't some shortcut to college success. I make no promises or guarantees. Your embrace and use of the concepts will determine what you'll get out of it. That's what college is as well. The more you engage your classes, professors, and fellow students, the more success you'll enjoy.

Don't think you need to memorize or even retain all you're about to read. Try to grasp concepts rather than details. By reading this now, you'll gain greater confidence as you head toward your college adventure. This little book should go with you so you can review a section if needed.

Why should you read this book? Because mastering college is a precursor for mastering life. Somewhere between our late teens and early twenties, many of us participate in something that sets the stage for the rest of our lives. For so many, this something is going to college, but the majority of students claw and fight their way toward graduation because they don't know how to manage their college experience. I'll show you how in this book.

Why not learn these simple skills that reduce stress and produce results? It works for college and will work for you in life.

Ultimately, it's about grit. Angela Duckworth said, "Enthusiasm is common. Endurance is rare."[1] Thousands of people begin college every year. Many earn a degree. But few master their college experience in such a way that it transforms their lives and sets them on a course for greatness. Do you have the grit and determination for greatness?

---

[1] Duckworth, Angela. *Grit: The Power of Passion and Perseverance*. Toronto, Ontario: HarperCollins, 2016.

2.

SMALL BITES

We have a common saying in our house: pursue excellence. Whether it's school, work, sports, music, volunteer service, or a hobby, do it with excellence. This pursuit forces goal-setting and careful planning. It requires the needed skills, or the acquirement of the skills, to do it well. Producing excellence means stopping and restarting if errors are encountered. The greatest thing about pursuing top-notch work is that after enjoying the satisfaction of a job well done, you gain confidence, because now you know you can do it again. Once you know your process, you might be able to do it faster, easier, and cheaper next time. It takes small steps to get there.

For example, I intend to write this book with excellence. If I didn't have that intention, I wouldn't waste my time. I've written five other books and now have a process in place to do it faster, easier, and cheaper than my first book. Granted, I may write a book that takes longer, requires more extensive research, and has higher creation costs, but the time, effort, and cost per word are more efficient because I've already done it. It may not necessarily be excellent in everyone's eyes, but I'll know that I pursued excellence, and offered my best work.

I wrote those five books one at a time, one writing session at a time. Starting with a single word each time, I wrote in small bites that became sentences, then paragraphs, then chapters. I have a goal of how much I want to write over time and track that success on a spreadsheet. Once the goal is set, I record each daily writing session as it grows from an outline to a book. This methodical approach produces quality work and makes large projects—such as a major paper or entire course—less daunting.

Most writers have a daily word count they adhere to. A novelist producing one book per year might have a daily word count of 500 words per day with weekends off. They write five days per week over eight months for their initial draft. The following months are for rewriting, editing, polishing, and publication. Then, they start all over again. This methodical approach not only gets the job done, but also makes the work palatable and less stressful, offering the proper time needed to make it excellent. This proven process produces quality work.

I use the example of writing a book because so many people want to write one yet most don't. They're concerned about the amount of work it will take or they simply fear failure. That's also a common reason people don't attend college—the fear of the work involved or the fear of failure. If you're reading this book, I suspect you know it's a lot of work and might be concerned about failure. If you take your work one step at a time and stick to the process, you won't fail. In fact, you'll likely do much better than you ever anticipated.

Ultimately, I'm hoping you'll buy into the concept that using a proven process, and performing each step well, delivers repeated success. That's how you'll handle all those syllabi coming your way. More on those in the next chapter, but first, we need to embrace the concept of small bites. Legendary Dallas Cowboys coach Tom Landry said that "Setting a goal is not the main thing. It is deciding how you will go about achieving it and staying with that plan."

Let's consider two lines of strategy to accomplish one goal. Let's make that goal an "A" in your first history course. The professor will likely require you to attend class, be prepared by reading the text that he'll lecture on, take quizzes and tests, and complete a writing project. First, take a deep breath. Rarely is anything major due on day one. Day one is about listening and absorbing instructions, thinking about the learning objectives of the course, and considering the value this new knowledge will bring you. It's similar to reading the preface of a book.

Strategy one is the power of addition. If you don't regularly do push-ups, you probably won't start with fifty. You might bang out fifteen or sixteen. Be satisfied with that and plan to add one per day. Guess how many you'll be able to do on day fifty. In the same way, don't bear the burden of the entire class on day one. You only have so much knowledge, but you can add to that knowledge a little every day and then you'll effortlessly master that final exam.

Think of other examples. No one reads the Bible or *Les Misérables* in one day. They read a little bit every day. Babies and toddlers don't learn to speak immediately. They pick up words and phrases over time. No one starts with calculus. You wouldn't dare take thermodynamics without a foundation in physics. You already have a lot of historical knowledge before that history class starts. Be thankful for that. Focus on that small bite you need to add each day.

Let's get practical. We'll discuss planning and calendar strategies later, but for now, think through an average three weeks in that course where you may have six classes, one quiz, one test, and 120 pages of reading. Use each class period to break this up into six pockets of time. Before class one, and let's say it's on Tuesday, you add sixty minutes on your calendar for Monday afternoon. You spend that time reviewing the previous class, reading twenty pages of text, taking a mock quiz, and memorizing items you think will be on the test.

This way, you're not burdening yourself with the whole semester, but taking that three-week period—leading up to a test, for example—to break it down into six small bites. During the bite, your phone is turned over, the room is either quiet or filled with white noise or music that helps you study, and the lighting is sufficient so there's no eye strain. No one, no thing, not even your daydreaming mind invades that "bite" time. I'm not suggesting sixty minutes is always enough, it's probably not, but the important thing is, you've devoted time to that bite. Navy SEALs endure a five-day crucible called Hell Week that has dozens of exercises—called evolutions—all to be done on four hours of sleep for the entire week. They're trained to only think of one evolution at a time. One bite at a time.

Strategy two is the power of expertise. Plan to be the class expert on that subject. I don't mean you challenge the professor or show off to your classmates. I mean that you plan to become an expert in History 101 among your peers. Be confident, not cocky. Be the one others ask for help on a particular point the professor made in class or on how to understand a historical event. If you're the "go-to," then you know that you've got this class down. Essentially, if you can almost teach it, you've got it down.

The beauty of this second strategy is that you'll eventually find a subject in which you'll want to not only practice expertise but also become the world's foremost authority. I once met a biologist who was passionate about earthworms. We were at a party and he dove right into a discussion about how they grow, where they live, and their contribution to the environment. He made it interesting because he told me things about the creatures that most biologists don't even know. His passion and enthusiasm sold me on the value of earthworms. Not everyone cares about earthworms, but his desire to become the world's foremost authority on earthworms forced him to develop the strongest of study skills. This is why professors have you write research papers. They want you to dig deep into a particular topic so you develop research skills. In *Outliers: The Story of Success*, Malcolm Gladwell shows how some became experts in their field by devoting 10,000 hours toward their craft. That's passion for sure, but all of them put in those hours over time, a few bites at a time.

Think of the Beach Boys' Brian Wilson. He's pursued creativity with a zeal unlike most. His bandmates and studio musicians stood by as he tinkered with instruments like a mad scientist when creating the song "Wouldn't It Be Nice." The song was a hit, topping the charts. What does Brian Wilson have to do with that History 101 course? Tinker, toil, and don't settle. Make it your own. Become the master of History 101. I know that sounds over the top, but you're pursuing excellence.

Mediocre students say things like, "That probably won't be on the test," or "I've probably studied enough," and then they move on to things that don't produce stellar grades. My answer to them is not necessarily to spend more time studying but to study more efficiently. I finished one history course with a 100.2 average thanks to three extra credit points. Here's the secret: I didn't spend any more time than all the students with averages in the 70s and 80s. I worked smarter, not harder. I had a goal to score the top grade in the class, and I succeeded.

NFL rushing leader Emmitt Smith wrote his goals down and placed them in a location he'd see every day. Some of his goals were to have no fumbles (pursuing excellence), to rush 125 yards per game (small bites), and to win the Super Bowl (team effort).

What are your goals? Write them down. Here are some you might consider: never miss class, get a 3.8 GPA, exercise four times per week, help one person every day. Whatever they are, write them down and read them every morning.

One of the last things I completed in academics was a biography for my master's thesis on a war hero known to few. I might know more about that person than anyone other than their family and a few others. I don't say that to brag but to explain how everything I learned about the power of addition and the power of expertise culminated into a thesis that earned an "A" and was completed early. I never had to pull an all-nighter or stress over deadlines. I followed my goal to earn a master's degree. I did it all with small bites. Smarter, not harder. Remember that.

Recommended Reading: Gladwell, Malcolm. *Outliers: The Story of Success*. New York, NY: Back Bay, 2013.

3.

SYLLABUS SHOCK

You've likely heard the term "syllabus shock." If not, I'll define it. It's that overwhelming fear you experience at the beginning of the semester when you realize how much work is ahead of you. You can't imagine how you'll understand all those concepts, read all those texts, write those research papers, and finish everything by the professor's deadlines. You don't even know where to begin. Fear not! Here's what you can do.

Think of a syllabus as a contract between you and the professor. It contains provisions that work in your favor, the professor's favor, and negotiable items. Professors have some freedom in designing their course, but they must conform to certain requirements for accreditation, university policy, and departmental goals. Let's break down a typical syllabus.

Some of this is mundane, but don't miss the fine print. You need to read every word of the course description and objectives. They give you the big picture of the course, the instructor's goals, and help you understand the rest of the syllabus. Don't be the student that goes through the motions frustrated and asking, "Why do I need to learn this?" Read each objective with three questions in mind. How does it feed into the course description? How will it help me in other courses? How can I use this knowledge in the future? Remember that line from earlier: "Get paid for what you know, not what you do."

Textbooks and materials typically fall into one of two categories: required and recommended. Don't assume you can get by without the required pieces. I don't presume that you'll need every page, but students that skip the required text usually have trouble. Do you need a new copy? Not necessarily. The syllabus may explain that you need a new, plastic-wrapped copy of a book with a code inside for online registration. If so, you may not want to open it until your professor confirms it's needed on the first day of class. Otherwise, used rentals are a nice option, or simply buy a used copy, making sure you have the correct edition. You can highlight or write notes and markings in those books.

Most professors know how costly textbooks are, so they'll be conscious. Bring only what's required on day one and then purchase the recommended resources later if needed. For example, the recommended text might be a handbook that you only need a few times and that can be found in the library. It may be material that's readily available online. Check with the campus bookstore to make sure anything you don't purchase will be in stock the first week of class. Not having every possible text on day one might cause you extra stress. If it does, purchase it but save your receipt so you can return it. On the other hand, some are more stressed by the huge stacks of unknown books that begin a semester.

The assignments section of the syllabus lays out your core workload with weighted percentages toward the final grade. This is the "meat" of the contract. You do a certain amount of work and are rewarded with a certain grade. An example might be:

Labs	10%
Quizzes	10%
Three Tests	20% each
Final Exam	20%

They might include some details. For example, there will be ten pop quizzes, but they'll drop two scores. In other words, they'll average your top eight scores for that 10%. It's not unusual for a professor to build in 10% for class participation. They base that grade on whether they think you're prepared, have read the material, and whether you raise your hand on occasion. That's an easy 10%, so don't miss out on that.

Think of these percentages in terms of those small bites. Focus on earning a few points at a time. Students sometimes fall into the trap of hoping one good test or a solid last-minute research paper will save their grade. It rarely does. At best, it secures a "C" versus a "D." Consider each percentage as its own piece of a machine. The lab piece needs to run at almost perfect efficiency for the test piece to run well. Each piece working in synchronicity. Don't think of the lab grade as an insignificant part of your final grade. Consider it the difference between an A and a B.

Grading criteria for research papers are not always as clear as they are for tests. For example, some professors will have you complete research papers piecemeal. They'll have you submit a synopsis and outline to make sure you've chosen the correct subject and have a plan. It's rare, but they may ask for a rough draft and to read a sample. If they don't do either of these, ask the professor for some time during their office hours to show them your plan and a sample paragraph. Make sure you know their standard for content, sourcing, formatting, grammar, and spelling. I'll devote an entire chapter to writing research papers, but I'm using this as an example of how to go beyond the syllabus. Don't guess about these requirements. Know them for certain.

This next subject is where you sometimes have some room for negotiation. Does the professor allow extra credit? If they do, don't even consider this to be optional. Immediately add it to your required list. If they don't offer it outright in class, ask about it early in the semester. Professors are used to struggling students making a desperate plea the last few weeks of the semester. Explain that you don't expect to need it, but you want to pursue every option to enhance your knowledge of the subject and ensure a top grade. I'm not suggesting you be manipulative, but rather, go to them with a genuine goal in mind. Not all of them will accept, but some will. I know, because it's worked for me. Extra credit assignments typically have some flexibility in that you can pick subjects for extra reading or writing that interest you. Most professors love eager students that are sincere in their requests.

The syllabus will be loaded with two types of policy language. Some may be the professor's standard on late work, helpful hints on where to find research material, and instructions for online access for the course. The long section has departmental or university standards on plagiarism and student conduct. These may be repetitive, but you need to know the rules. Ignorance will not be an excuse.

Professors always list their contact information and office hours. On day one, create a contact in your phone with this info. You're going to need it. Remember, the syllabus is a contract, so you need to know how to reach the other party to make sure you're complying with it. I'm not suggesting you make a daily visit or stop by only to chit-chat. Rather, take advantage of the professor's office hours when you need to solve misunderstandings or to ensure you're on the right track with an assignment.

What if the syllabus changes? It rarely does, but a class closure due to weather, a professor realizing the class needs extra work, or other reasons might cause professors to change the contract. Make sure you're tuned into every possible way they might communicate that. Don't be that student complaining that something on the test wasn't covered in class. Professors may include test material from lectures, textbooks, online resources, labs, emails, or a post on their office door. So know all avenues of communication, and catch up if you miss something.

A large section may lay out the class schedule, what will be covered, required reading, and the testing method. Many courses will move this information to the online portal with details about each assignment that you can download to your device and calendar software. I highly recommend you do that and build in those bite-sized study times we discussed earlier. Most software easily allows you to assign a recurring event. Treat your studies like a job. Set a routine of waking at the same time each day and doing some work for each class, each day. Yes, you may have to do some work on the weekend. Below, I've included a sample of what might go on a calendar over two weeks for one class.

Mon	Tue	Wed	Thurs	Fri	Sat	Sun
2:00 pm–3:00 pm HIS 101 Prep	10:00 am–11:20 am HIS 101 Class	2:00 pm–3:00 pm HIS 101 Prep	10:00 am–11:20 am HIS 101 Class	3:00 pm–4:00 pm HIS 101 Reading		
2:00 pm–3:00 pm HIS 101 Prep	10:00 am–11:20 am HIS 101 Class	2:00 pm–3:00 pm HIS 101 Prep	10:00 am–11:20 am HIS 101 Class	3:00 pm–4:00 pm HIS 101 Reading	11:30am–1:30 pm HIS 101 Writing	

A few observations. Common wisdom is that you should spend two hours outside of class for every one hour in class. I don't doubt that at all. In this instance, I scheduled a little less outside of class time, but that might change two weeks into the semester once I've understood my workload. Another class may require you to spend three hours of study time for every class hour. At the beginning of the semester, fill your calendar with slots for every lecture and each prep, reading, and writing session. You can tweak it later. This is exactly like creating a budget. You're given so much time in a week, so spend it wisely. The most important thing is having a plan. Most students never build a calendar. Some put their class times on there. A few also place intentional study times there and stick to the plan. Be that last type. That's a winning student.

Notice the time on Saturday devoted to writing. Over time, you'll likely develop a style of academic writing and you'll know how long you need to write a paper of a certain size. I found that if I had done my pre-writing research, the required reading, and written an outline, I could finish one page per hour. After a few Saturdays, that dreaded research paper is finished, and it has the needed quality as opposed to one written during an all-nighter that required shortcuts and shoddy work.

Your calendar will also include all of your non-coursework activities, such as your work schedule if you have a job, exercise, club meetings, and free time. Am I suggesting you put "free time" on the calendar? Not necessarily, but make sure you plan some time to relax and recharge. That might be on Sunday or another day. Loads of time management and calendar software can help you plan for work and relaxation. Your school likely has these for free but you can find others online. I use Google Calendar and know it will work for this. Setting up a calendar is a week-one must for you. It is the antidote for syllabus shock. You can adjust it over the next several weeks as you learn your own strengths and weaknesses.

Many calendars allow for color-coding so you can change the color as you complete a task. They might even have percentages or some other marker to track progress by the day, week, or semester. Use what motivates you. I heard of one student that placed an M&M on each page she needed to read. When she finished the page, she rewarded herself with that candy. Maybe, for you, finishing a morning task means a walk with your favorite podcast or audiobook. A full day completed means you catch up on a show or do some gaming.

If you're reading this early enough, I strongly encourage taking a few dual credit courses during high school. They help you experience college-level work once or twice before committing to full-time study at a university. It's also nice to transfer a few classes toward your major, and you will have saved money from the likely lower tuition rate of a community college. As a plus, you can experience the shock of only one syllabus, play with how to move it to a calendar, and learn from how that contract plays out.

At the beginning of your first semester, take every orientation the college offers. If living on campus, clear a full day after you've moved in, but before classes start, so you can relax or go see a movie. Get your parking pass and student ID a day or more before class starts. Walk the campus and find the lecture halls or classrooms for your courses so you can plan your walking route and the time it takes to move from one class to another. All those little things reduce stress so that once that first class starts, these distractions will be behind you.

A final note on preparing for syllabus shock: You should be meeting with your advisor every semester before registering for the next semester. They'll make sure you're on track and taking the right classes in the right order, but just as important, they'll help you find a balanced approach.

Engineering majors might take calculus, physics, chemistry, English, and government in one semester and do well. If you're a humanities major, you may not want to take math and science in the same semester. Advisors can help you lay out your entire four years of college, by course, by semester, with a few place holders for electives or shifting a class due to availability. They know what classes will or won't be offered each semester. That's their job. Use them.

Students have survived syllabus shock for decades. You don't need to panic. You have a plan. That's the key. Work smarter, not harder.

4.

TESTMASTER OR TEACHER'S PET

A show in the late 1950s, called *Leave It to Beaver*, had a character named Eddie Haskell. Eddie treated Beaver, the young protagonist of the show, with disrespect and called him "Squirt." His two-faced demeanor usually manifested itself when Beaver's parents encountered him. He'd pretend to show respect for the young Beaver while scheming behind the scenes. No one likes a guy like that, but it made for great comedy. The character is now a metaphor for duplicity. Don't be an Eddie Haskell. Professors know this behavior the moment they see it.

I'm sure you think "teacher's pet" is pejorative. But there are those students who unwittingly curry favor with the teacher because they're good students. They get excited when the teacher announces a pop quiz because they're prepared. Other students look down on them over jealousy or pettiness. There is a diplomatic way to establish a relationship with the professor, avoid the Eddie Haskell comparison, and not isolate yourself from your classmates. And, by the way, there's nothing wrong with excitement over a quiz or test that you're prepared for.

It all starts with the right professor. You may think you don't have a choice, but many times you do. Most classes are taught by more than one person. A quick internet search or asking your fellow students will give you loads of information on a professor's background, how other students have fared with them, and whether they might be a good fit for you. Remember, you're entering into a contract with them. Take the time for due diligence. Ignore the few students who are likely complaining because they received a bad grade and focus on comments about how the professor prepares students for tests or how they feel the professor made them successful in the class.

Are they funny? You may or may not like that. Do their tests rely heavily on the lecture or more on reading? Do they only read from slides or are they passionate about teaching? Would you rather be taught in a lecture with heavy note-taking or in a way that depends more on outside reading?

Now that you think you're matched with the right professor, I want you to think like a professor. Don't consider them an adversary; think of them as a partner invested in your academic success. Most of them chose this career because they love to teach and shape young minds. They're passionate about their specialty and hope you're interested in the subject as well. They know some sitting before them resent having to take the required class, but they hope they can still give them something of value. Put yourself in their place. What kind of student would you want to teach?

Let's consider two examples: math and history. "Why do I need algebra?" You've likely heard it dozens of times and may have asked it yourself. If you have, I'm suggesting you appreciate this class anyway by considering other elements it has to offer. From a practical standpoint, there are no major papers due or long reading assignments. I'll include a whole chapter on math later, but for now, think about how math helps with the daily habit of critical thinking. Math exercises your brain. Typically, non-technical degrees only require three to six credit hours of math. College Algebra or Finite Mathematics will be one course, but consider other options your school may offer, such as Business Math, Math for Liberal Arts Majors, or Philosophy of Logic.

What if you're more of a science type and don't appreciate all those names and dates? History isn't just about that. It's about events fitting into people's lives. Focus on the stories. The greatest history professor I ever had would walk up and down the aisles between our seats telling stories. For the tests, we had to know twenty-five people or events and write something about each. We had no problem recalling two or three significant details for each because we remembered the stories and how they fit into the bigger historical narrative. What if your professor doesn't tell stories? Make your own and "paint" pictures in your mind. Stories have a beginning, a middle, and an end.

Here's an example. Over a year before the signing of the Declaration of Independence, British troops marched toward Concord to confiscate arms stored by local patriot militia. Riders such as Paul Revere warned the locals that the British were coming from Boston. Two lamps in the Old North Church signaled that the British were coming by water. The first battle of the Revolutionary War began. The Patriots won and drove the British back to Boston. That's a really short version, but it's told in story form. Can you see the British in boats? Revere riding? The two lamps? Notice there are no dates. However, you probably know the Declaration of Independence was signed on July 4, 1776. It's good to know that the Battle of Concord took place on April 19, 1775, but understanding that the war started well before declaring independence gives you the story chronology, making you better able to hold on to the dates.

That required history course will give you some valuable skills in research and writing, useful in nearly any career field. You'll gain knowledge of how the world works. Math teaches you to think. Don't resent these courses. Embrace them. Imagine how that attitude will shine through to your professor. Professors are convinced of their class's value for your success in college and life. They've seen the fruit of their specialty benefit people, business, or science. The last thing you want to show is disdain for something they're passionate about.

Inevitably, right before or after class, a few students will gather and commence with a gripe session.

A girl walks to her seat and drops her backpack. "How's anyone supposed to remember all this? There's no way I'm passing this test."

The guy sitting next to her rolls his eyes. "I hate this class."

You have a few choices. You could join their chorus of complaints, but that's a bad decision. You could ignore them. That's acceptable but may rob you of a valuable opportunity. What if you offer to help them? That's a win-win strategy. If you spend some time studying with them, showing them your attitude, explaining how you've had success in the class, you may just help them in more ways than one. Practically, they'll do better in that class, but you might help make them a better student overall. In addition, you'll learn more by teaching the material. It may make sense to form a study group that meets weekly to fill in some gaps you missed. Imagine how much you'd benefit from leading a study group. This will force you not only to master the material but to have it mastered by a scheduled time. That's winning in college. Now, if they continue to complain, act like knuckleheads, and drain your mental energy with a bad attitude, don't feel guilty about abandoning that one opportunity.

Professors know when you've come to class prepared. Most of them are not out to trick you or find the most arcane topic to quiz you about in front of the whole class. If your professor likes to ask the class questions, I don't suggest throwing your hand up and answering every one even if you know the answer. Your classmates may resent you. However, I do suggest throwing your hand up often and trying to get in at least two answers or comments per class. Keep your answers brief and on point. If you're able to tackle most of the questions asked in class, then you'll know you're preparing appropriately.

As you do your pre-class work, think of things the professor might ask and think about how you'd answer them. Preparing for an oral test is a skillful way to master the material. Your brain will more easily store that information for quick recall. Let's imagine you're studying the digestive system for a biology class. The professor probably won't ask you to spell esophagus. Steer away from things that aren't relevant. Instead, try to notice two or three unique things about each organ and how the organs relate to each other. Think of how a bite of steak moves from one organ to the next. That's big-picture stuff, and it's the type of information you'll need to understand, and participate in, the lecture.

Use this same strategy during class lectures. Always think of how the subject matter applies to a greater topic or how it correlates to something else. The more you connect things to each other and think about how they relate, the stronger the likelihood you'll retain and understand the information. Don't simply jot down everything the professor says. When you copy it down, do so with a purpose in mind. Here's a sample from history:

The professor states, "Germany invaded Poland on September 1, 1939, but Japan didn't attack the United States until December 7, 1941."

We could write that down verbatim, but the following is quicker and captures the information you need:

- Germany invaded Poland 9-1-39
- Japan attacked US 12-7-41

There's nothing wrong with jotting that down, and I suspect everyone reading this already knew the second fact. But did you know the first one about Germany invading Poland? Here's where you correlate. Americans, especially, forget that World War II started over two years before the attack on Pearl Harbor. In fact, Japan had been at war with China since 1937 and President Franklin Roosevelt took steps to stop Japanese aggression in the Far East.

Let's think big picture on these facts. War raged in other parts of the world. The United States held an isolationist stance but aided its allies though several policies. The world was at war for years. The attack on Pearl Harbor drew the United States into the conflict. Germany, an ally of Japan and member of the Axis, declared war on the United States. That's how those names and dates fit in. Hopefully, your professor explained the big picture. Your notes should look more like this, like a story, as if you're telling the story to someone else. It's much stronger for comprehension and retention.

Test yourself constantly.
Q: Who invaded Poland?
A: Germany.
Q: Why did Germany declare war on the United States?
A: Because they were a member of the Axis with Japan.
Q: Why did Japan attack the United States?
A: Due to American policies in the Far East.
Remember how you learned to do this in elementary algebra?

$X - 2 = 1$
Solve for x.

Add 2 to both sides.
$x - 2 + 2 = 1 + 2$
$x = 3$
Now plug in 3 for the x.
$3 - 2 = 1$

That back and forth with nearly any subject creates strong connections for your learning. Earlier, I suggested remembering history as a story. Learn the story and then test yourself on it.

My notes are full of arrows and other marks that connect related points. Create graphs or diagrams even for non-technical subjects. Imagine you had to teach the lecture at a later date. What notes would you need to take to be able to properly explain the topic?

You may prefer to go back and highlight with one or more colors. If you take notes on your laptop, it's easier to go back through after class, clean up the text, and use a variety of tools to mark the material. It's a great way to review what you just learned. Assuming you own your textbook, read with a pen or highlighter in hand. Create your own system of marks for things that stand out, that you suspect may correlate, that you have a question about, or which you think will be on the test. The key here is to interact with the material rather than let it go in one ear and out of the other.

If your professor allows it, you might consider recording the lecture so you can listen to it as you walk, do laundry, or review your notes. If they have a web-based course, they may grant you access to the online lectures recorded in a previous semester. You may not need to listen to the entirety of each lecture; just fast forward to the part you need. In addition, we live in an age where we can find a video online to explain just about anything.

This type of reading preparation and note-taking ensures you're ready for that pop quiz. A lot of students fall into the trap of putting too much stock in that sentence on some syllabi that says, "The two lowest quiz scores will be dropped." As we discussed earlier, that means, for example, that though the professor plans for ten pop quizzes, they will only average the top eight scores. Many students have a passive attitude on every quiz, thinking it could always be dropped. They end up with poor scores on all of them. Aim for a top score on every quiz. I'll give you a few reasons: You'll be better prepared for tests because the professor has essentially given you practice test questions. You have less stress knowing your quiz average is solid. You'll develop an attitude of aiming for strong scores on every assignment from quizzes, to papers, to labs, to tests.

This is a good time to explain the broken windows theory. Most people, when they see an abandoned building, wouldn't consider throwing a rock and breaking a window. However, when several windows are already broken, many will follow suit and try to break one. That's the slippery slope of not preparing for a quiz or skipping some required reading.

If your professor ever says, "You may see this again," they're telling you it's most likely on the test. So know that thing forward and backward. I know you wish they'd tell you all the test answers but at least they're emphasizing something you need to know for that class. Many professors will hold a test review session on the material prior to test day. You never want to miss that class because they'll likely cover something you may have missed or clarify something that you had misunderstood. Some students think, "I'll probably be able to figure it out once I see the test." I doubt it. I've tried that before. It's a failing attitude.

Real test preparation starts early, from the first day of reading the text or taking notes, or from those first labs. When you're test prepping every time you think about the class, you won't settle for "I'll figure that out later" or otherwise ignore a confusing concept. Listen, learn, practice, and know on a daily basis as you absorb that course. Don't wait until the eve of the test to cram, but prepare over time in small bites. It's so much easier.

Diligent students occasionally evaluate themselves. Let's say that six weeks into the semester, on a Friday afternoon, you take time to assess what your grade will likely be, up to that point. In five courses, you'd have two that are solid A's, in one class it could be an A or B, in a fourth a solid B, and in one class, you're in jeopardy of falling to a C. Make a list of your classes. What's one thing you can do in each of those solid A courses to maintain that? What are three things you can do to move that A or B to the solid A column? List four things that could get that B to an A, and finally, think of five things you can do to destroy that potential C and make it an unquestionable A.

Here are some examples of what those "things" can be: re-read a chapter, read ahead, do another edit on the paper before turning it in, review old quizzes and tests, plan to study with a stronger student in that course, review homework, watch a video that covers a teaching point, listen to a podcast or a lecture on the topic, visit your professor during office hours, ask them for ideas to bump up your grade, ask for extra credit, visit the departmental help center such as the math lab, and anything else that will enhance your knowledge. Some of these might take twenty minutes and some might take an hour. You might not do all of that every Friday, but you might do one or two classes each Friday.

If you haven't guessed by now, this chapter isn't really about that stereotypical teacher's pet. Nobody likes that two-faced rascal who attempts to curry favor with the professor. That's a given. Some don't like the student who's excelling. Don't mind those haters but also keep your pride in check. Your job is to pursue excellence while maintaining your humility. You're mastering college by managing your time and the way you process information.

5.

READ FASTER WHILE RETAINING MORE

Why read faster? Why not take your time and enjoy the reading? There's certainly nothing wrong with relaxing while diving into a novel. However, college requires you to read a tremendous amount of material. There are times you'll want to absorb information in a timely manner but still understand what you've read. Learning the skill we're about to cover will reap a huge savings in the time you spend reading.

Speed reading carries a number of connotations. Plenty of legitimate courses teach you how to read faster while comprehending more. Simply stated, that's what you want: speed and comprehension. Some are scams and promise you'll read ten times faster after one lesson for three easy payments of $19.99. They're gimmicks that will cause you to retain less and waste your time. The word "speed" tickles the ears, but I'm going to give you several steps that will make you a more efficient reader, and speed is only a small part of it.

A quick internet search will reveal those boasting reading speeds of thousands of words per minute. I don't doubt a few savants are capable of that, but most who claim that are scanning and not grasping much of the material. Let's focus on the typical person.

When I started a graduate program, the school offered a reading course over three weeks of the first semester. They tested me at the beginning, and I read at 320 WPM with 60% comprehension. I improved on week two and by week three scored at 585 WPM with 80% comprehension. Essentially, I doubled my reading speed while absorbing more. Currently, I read non-fiction at 600 WPM with great retention. I read fiction a little slower when there's a lot of back and forth dialogue.

For the rest of this chapter, I'll be referring to physical books, but most of the concepts apply to ebooks and online reading as well. Before we start reading, let's pick the right venue. Some of your studies require you to sit at a desk with a computer, to find a well-lit area where you can spread out several papers, or to work in a lab. When you study, you can choose to have white noise, music, or total quiet. You might like the lights dimmed. You may want people around or no humans in the vicinity. When it comes to studying, it's important you find a regular spot that is your "office." Reading, however, offers a chance for different spots, since you're not shackled to a desk or a lab. I love to read in public places such as a coffee shop or a park bench. Find your own spots and own them.

A short note on audiobooks. If you're a strong auditory learner, as I am, you may find opportunities to consume the material in that format. I listen at double or triple speed depending on the narrator. If you think about it, it's similar to reading words on a page faster. If I'm focused, I can handle the information at a great speed and retain it. It probably won't be that biology or math text, but other classes may allow you to read or listen in any format that works. Depending on the subject, I sometimes retain more information from audio than physical reading. Most of you may need your eyeballs to see that word or how that character's name is spelled, so I'm certainly not telling you that audio is better, just that you may benefit from trying it.

Once you have that new book in hand, don't start on page one. Let's make sure we've grasped what we're about to read and avoid future distractions. We call this previewing a book. Read everything on the front and back covers and inside the dust jacket. Those are the things the author most wants you to know about their book. A lot of marketing work went into the book's appearance and cover content in hopes that it would persuade you to buy the book, and that persuasion clues you into what you'll gain. If available, check out reviews online. Read one review under each star rating, but maybe read a few more with three and four stars. They usually offer the best perspective.

Now, look through the front matter—that's all the pages before chapter one—particularly the table of contents. Think about how each chapter relates to the synopsis and thesis of the book, which you likely gleaned from the cover. In the front matter, is there a foreword? This is usually written by someone with related expertise or by an associate of the author. It's your chance to find out what someone familiar with the material has to say about the book. Most readers skip over the preface (which is written by the author) thinking it's only a summary or an unneeded introduction. Read it! The author is telling you why they wrote the book, why you need to read it, and how it will bring you value. It's basically a longer, more detailed synopsis.

Now, flip through the main text and look through any photos and read the captions, making your way to the back matter. Is there a glossary, appendix, or bibliography? I'm not necessarily advising you to read that, but do familiarize yourself with it for quick reference later. Once you're in the flow of reading, you don't want to pause and spend time on front and back matter. Previewing the book takes minutes and aids in your comprehension because you know exactly where you're headed. I realize much of this doesn't apply to fiction, but you can go ahead and look through the front and back matter of novels too; it won't hurt. This preview is done before the semester begins so that when that syllabus is in your hand, you know how that book complements the syllabus. If wrapped and not returnable when opened, it may be worth unwrapping to complete the preview.

You've found the right reading spot and familiarized yourself with the book, so let's start reading. Each of those speed-reading courses will suggest different ways to read faster, but, essentially, you're not scanning, rather you're grouping a few words at a time. You move left to right and grasp those word groupings, typically three or four per sentence or line. At first, you'll read as you've always done, scrolling across every word, but soon you'll be bumping from one grouping to another. You don't need to stop on every "the" or "and." Your eye sees the word "the" and in a fraction of a second processes it with the noun after it. It's similar to "he said" in fiction. You don't really read that or need to read that. Your mind processes it as if it were punctuation. Think about it. You're finishing these sentences without reading or saying "period."

Here's an example from chapter one:

College builds ~~your~~ mind. ~~The~~ building blocks ~~are those~~ courses. ~~Learn to~~ find value ~~in~~ every block. ~~This little~~ book teaches ~~you~~ dozens ~~and~~ dozens ~~of~~ ways ~~to~~ make ~~that~~ easier, enjoyable, ~~and more~~ efficient. ~~It's about~~ working smarter, ~~not~~ harder. ~~You might~~ hear ~~that~~ phrase again.

The words I've struck through are those you'll naturally focus less on during the bumping and grouping. They're important, but your eyes saw them much like peripheral vision and connected them to the other words. Also, notice there are about four to five groups per line. There's no official list as to what words are glanced over and how groups are formed. This will come naturally. One might suggest you'll retain less by reading in this way, and that's possible, but most improve their retention because their reading is so much more focused.

You might want to use a pen or your finger at first to keep you constantly moving from one line to another. Don't backtrack. Keep moving. Don't stop at the bottom of the page. Move quickly to the top of the next page and keep reading. As you get to the bottom of the right page, get ready to turn the page and keep reading. Keep it moving while constantly connecting concepts to the goal of the section or chapter. At the end of the chapter, ask yourself how what you just read connects to the book's premise as a whole and leads into the next chapter. Put yourself on a timer with the goal of finishing a certain number of words or pages in that time. This will help you manage your time and give yourself a little motivation to keep the pace. After about ten minutes, you'll know whether a particular book takes you one page per minute or four pages per minute. That really helps with your planning.

I suggest keeping a record of your reading as you develop this skill. You can count the average number of words per page so you can calculate your words per minute, or just use the page-per-minute method. If you find that you are reading a particular book at a pace of 2.0 pages per minute, have a goal to improve to 2.5 over the next three reading sessions with the ultimate goal of reaching 3.0 pages per minute for that type of book. I'm not suggesting you'll top out, but we all have a limit where we move from speed reading with retention to simply scanning with less retention.

If you're not progressing, ask yourself if you're finding yourself distracted, backtracking, stopping your pace, or altering your pace. Try to hyper-focus for a few minutes and keep a firm pace. Over time, you'll develop a whole new reading habit. Think of this in terms of running. You've been walking and you don't really want to sprint. Rather, you're looking for that jogging pace that gets you a nice distance over time.

If you're reading with a pen or highlighter, consider a marking system as mentioned in the section about note-taking. I'll give you a few examples. I don't highlight whole words or sentences, I quickly touch an important word or stroke across it. If I want to take note of more than just one word or two, I make a mark at the edge of the page or circle the grouping, sentence, or paragraph. Don't slow yourself down by neatly "painting within the lines." With my pen, I simply make a little mark like "<" or ">" for something I think I'll need later, or as I said, I may circle the whole area. I also keep a few 3 × 5 sticky notes in the back of the book where I can quickly jot down a page number and short note on why it's important if needed. Remember, a lot of your academic reading is test prep or research for writing. If you're reading specifically for a research paper, print a miniature copy of the outline and keep it in the back of the book or use it for your bookmark. Then, you can jot down a relevant page number next to that bullet point on the outline for reference later.

What happens when you come across a word you don't know? I really don't want you to stop reading, but I do want you to know that word. Hold your pen or finger on that spot, reread that sentence and consider the context. If that doesn't work, quickly look it up. If you know that access to an electronic device to look up a word will cause you to start checking social media, write the page number and unknown word in your notes. Later, go back to the line and make sure you see how the definition fits. Then, try to work that word into your vocabulary so you'll further process knowledge of it and retain it. A great byproduct of reading is building a robust vocabulary while avoiding verbosity. See what I did there?

Much of what we've discussed can apply to ebooks or reading on a computer screen. Play with the settings for background color, font, size, and navigation on your e-reader. Many have highlighting features and some will auto scroll to keep you on pace. You can still read with your finger, pen, or stylus.

You're going to have to read about subjects that you'd never consider exploring in your free time. We all read for different reasons: pleasure, work, school, information, or self-help. Your attitude will determine how hard you make this. I try to find value in everything I read. I look for themes, heroes, emotion, history, and ideology. That may sound dramatic, but it has always helped me appreciate reading, not resent it. I find reading more interesting and retain more with that attitude.

I make no guarantees that your reading speed will triple after reading this chapter. I've touched on some basic concepts to improve your reading speed, but it takes practice. I encourage you to take a speed-reading course, but make sure their promises are realistic and that they also focus on improved comprehension, not just speed. Over time, you'll be able to pick up a book, thumb through a few pages, and know you can knock out fifty pages in thirty minutes.

Along the way, someone may recommend *How to Read a Book* by Mortimer Adler. I don't list it as recommended reading, but I consider it a strong resource. In particular, if you're an English major focusing on epic poetry, you may find his teaching on this valuable. Those engaged in classical reading might consider it a must-have text. I know many scoff at a book about how to read a book; however, why wouldn't everyone assigned thousands of pages to read find it worthy to spend a short time learning how to make their reading more efficient?

Mastering reading will go a long way in helping you master college. I once hated reading but now consume about sixty books each year. I read fiction and non-fiction on a wide variety of topics. You may not have that same passion, but I hope you'll appreciate the value of reading efficiently.

Before we move on to the next topic, here's another way to make your college reading life a little easier: get ahead of the reading prior to the semester. You can do this for any subject, but you'll likely find more motivation to do it with subjects in your major area of study. Assuming you've registered, ask professors about the required reading, and try to get your textbooks early. Professors might share with you specific pages to read or the title of a novel that'll be required. Over the break or in the summer leading up to the fall semester, you can do all the previewing and read the first several chapters. The beginning of the semester is busy enough, so why not get a jump-start? Following is a sample email you can send.

> Dr. McHenry,
>
> I'm taking PHIL 3300 next semester and am curious if you could send me the syllabus or a list of the required texts so I can get a head start on the reading over the holidays.
>
> Thanks,
> Cate Smith

I've done this many times, and they almost always respond with the syllabus or at least the instructions for the assigned text.

6.

THE NO-GIMMICK WAY TO MEMORIZE

I told you in chapter one that most of these skills will work for you in college and in life. This skill might be at the top of the list and can save you hours of study time. Yes, hours. As I did with reading efficiently, I'll touch on some basic concepts and give you some working solutions that you can use as early as today. I'll also recommend a resource at the end to truly harness this skill to its full potential like a professional speaker, top-tier salesman, or CIA agent would.

Here's a quick example from my graduate degree in history for which the university required passing a comprehensive exam. The four-hour-long test consisted of essay questions across six of the courses we had taken. That meant we had to know and write about major components from each course. Many of my fellow students spent weeks studying for the exam. I spent about one hour one day, and then thirty minutes a day over the next three days. That's right, just under three hours, and I easily passed.

Before I explain the main system I used, and continue to use, know there are many out there. You probably learned a song with rhyming as a child to help you remember something. Nothing wrong with that. There's always rote memory, that is, committing something to memory by repetition. It works and sometimes is the only solution, but it can take much longer. Acrostics are nice, as are acronyms, like FOIL from Algebra which reminds you how to multiply binomials. Do you remember what FOIL stands for? First, Outer, Inner, Last. I still remember, although I haven't needed to solve a binomial in quite some time.

I've also already talked about "linking" or "chain" techniques, like when I told you to connect those World War II concepts about Germany and Japan. It's very much like telling a story, while making sure each element of the story has strong links from one to the next. Here's an example that might apply in a business course. What are the four keys of marketing? Price, product, promotion, and place. That can be difficult to remember because they all start with "p." Let's write a linking story. Mom gave me a half-off-the-**price** coupon for the grocery store's newest **product**: Acme ice cream. The store is offering this **promotion** to draw more customers to their **place** of business. This works because it's a memorable story, it has all the elements that need to be memorized, and the elements actually represent what they do.

The ancient Greeks and Romans used a system called the Memory Palace, and it still works today. That's the main system I suggest you learn. Essentially, you're taking the thing you want to memorize and placing it in a location you've predetermined. Think of the house you lived in the longest, and create ten locations within it. The first might be the dining room table, second is the kitchen sink, third, your dad's favorite chair, and so on. Those are "hard" locations you'll use over and over. After a few tries, you won't even have to think about which one is number six, for example.

Place the first thing you want to memorize in location one. You need to make it vivid. Add color, action, sound, and even something silly. Let's say it's George Washington. Place him sitting at location one, the dining room table, in a bright red suit and sneezing. In the second location, place the Declaration of Independence, but imagine it's dipping in and out of the kitchen sink with the words falling off. For the third, Thomas Jefferson is sitting in your father's chair. He's writing and then crumbling paper and tossing into a trashcan. Sound silly? I know, but it works. The vivid action and connection to location are the keys.

Right now, think of ten locations you can use. Now, place the following ten things in those locations: A paintbrush, a coffee cup, love, Elvis Presley, pumpkins, the sun, the number twelve, anger, a monkey, and Las Vegas. For each one, give it lots of color, sound, and an action, maybe even something silly. That paintbrush might be placed on your TV. It's giant, painting in blue, and working so hard it breaks with a loud pop. Only take about ten seconds and then move on to the next item. It's important you think of your own action to make it more memorable. After you memorize the third item, review the first two. Do that again after you get to the seventh. Once you've memorized all ten, go through the list forward and backward. Yes, backward. You're simply walking through your list in reverse order. After some practice, you can easily associate an item with number six or nine. This list is only for practice, and obviously you won't care to memorize these items forever. However, I've used my main location list hundreds of times. Our family has done this same exercise on road trips. Once we set up our Memory Palaces, we quiz each other. If children can do this, I know you can.

With some practice, you'll be able to memorize ten things in a couple of minutes, memorize them once, and be done. I'm not suggesting they'll be memorized forever. You'd have to review them on occasion for that. However, this works well for things you want to know for a test in a day or two. You'll spend fifteen minutes, "walking" through your locations over the next day or two. Your classmate will spend a few frustrating hours cramming the day before. Which one would you rather do?

For that comprehensive exam, I created over one hundred locations. I used my current home, and each room became a major element. I used my kid's playroom for the Battle of Waterloo. I needed to remember seven major points and placed them on seven items in that room. I memorized that event once in under two minutes. After an hour, I had filled my house with military history.

Another option is to use locations in your neighborhood or town. Location one is your mailbox, two is the park, three is the big white house on the corner, and four the grocery store. Make it something familiar.

Two-time USA Memory Champion Ron White is no savant. He's a normal guy but considers himself a brain athlete and trains to harness the brain's power. He's taking his training to an astronomical level. He has a traveling memory wall where he writes out, from memory, the rank, first name, and last name of 2,400 of those who gave the ultimate sacrifice in Afghanistan. That's over 7,000 words. How does he do it? He has 2,400 locations in his Memory Palace. You may not want to take it to that level, but I hope that shows you the power of this skill.

The Memory Palace doesn't work for everything. Learning a foreign language takes a ton of practice, but many times you can find English cognates—foreign words with similar origins. For example, the Italian word *situazione* has the same origins as "situation." That one's easy. Now, take the French word *gaspiller*, which means "to waste." Imagine your mom pouring *gas* from a hose but missing the tank as it *spills* on the ground. "What a waste," she says. Again, create images. They're powerful.

I'm a big fan of mnemonics. In eighth grade, my teacher noticed several of us misspelling the word "separate" as "seperate." He wrote it correctly on the board and said, "Don't you see that little rat eating the apple?" For apple, he circled the first "a." I never write that word without hearing him say that, seeing him do that, and imagining a rat eating that apple (the "a"). Like the mind palace, this mnemonic is vivid, has action, and even has sound. It took him a few seconds to show us, and I remember that in a split-second whenever I use that word.

Of all the reading or courses I've recommended, none are more important than Ron White's memory course. If I were teaching a college course on "mastering college," I'd make this required material. I love how he teaches in small bites. You'll also learn how to remember the names of those you meet and memorize a long series of numbers. He also has a course on speed reading. He's saved me hundreds of hours, and he can for you as well.

Ron's course is a force multiplier. For every lesson you complete, you'll easily get back that time in hours saved from rote memorization. This chapter's a teaser for the massive amount of potential your mind can achieve. Imagine standing before your classmates for a presentation or giving a speech without notes. It's a fun skill you'll use the rest of your life.

Recommended Course: Ron White's Black Belt Memory at www.blackbeltmemory.com

7.

THE QUICK AND CLEAN GUIDE TO WRITING THOSE PAPERS

Take the library tour! Why start with that emphatic statement? Because the quickest and cleanest way to write quality research papers begins with research. That's why they're typically called "research" papers. Many a college student has stared at a blank screen wondering how they'll somehow write 1,500 words or five pages without resorting to "very, very, very, very, very, very, very, very, very" to complete their word count. They had a good idea and wrote a brief outline, but they ran out of things to write about a third of the way through. Panic sets in. It's happened to all of us.

Let's get back to the library. During your first semester, the library will offer orientation sessions for how to use their resources. I realize that seems outdated and that you can do much of your research on the internet. But, remember, the library offers so much more than books. They can show you how to narrow your research on substantive material rather than chasing down six books for one quote.

They can teach you how to use online resources and databases such as EBSCO (e.g. magazines) and JSTOR (e.g. academic journals) that are not available to the general public but which are free for you as a student. There, you might find a specific article on your topic that helps you build a paragraph or confirm a point you're trying to make. It's rewarding to find an old newspaper article or rare quotation that drives a point home. I loved using primary documents to strengthen my work, and I'll explain those in a bit.

Think of that initial orientation like a tutorial. The sixty minutes you spend on that will save you hours later. Remember what I've been saying? Work smarter, not harder. Tutorials are like reading the instructions. Nobody wants to do that. They want the quick path, but I'm confident that learning a proven research system will save you hours and reduce frustration.

Author Stephen King said, "If you don't have time to read, you don't have the time (or the tools) to write. Simple as that." It's true. Most of your research will involve reading, and we devoted the previous chapter to help you with that.

What other sources can you use? Class lectures are great sources since you're likely writing on a topic for that class. Most professors are happy for you to use them as a source, but keep in mind that they want you learning from resources outside of class as well. You can find podcasts on nearly every subject with interviews by leading experts. In fact, you can conduct your own interview in-person, by phone, or via email. Plenty of folks are eager to help out a college student who is genuinely interested in what the interviewee knows or witnessed.

Your professor may assign you to use a mix of primary versus secondary sources, and it's important you know the difference. It's likely that most of your papers in the past were sourced from secondary sources, such as non-fiction books, newspapers, or journal articles that were the result of an author's research. Your paper involved bringing those sources together to confirm or develop your thesis. Primary resources establish the origin of an event, not someone else's recounting of that origin. The following list is not exhaustive, but it will give you an idea of types of primary sources: interviews, government documents, letters, legal documents, experiments, or autobiographies. They're not always easy to find, but they're a much stronger source, so you should seek them out when you can.

Technology is your friend, and there are loads of software and apps at your disposal for both the research and the writing. I'm a big fan of cloud-based software that instantly saves my work and is accessible via any device, anywhere such as Google Drive, available when you sign up for a free Gmail account. I store all of my documents, notes, scans, and photos in folders and subfolders based on subject (or course). Save everything! You never know when you'll need to recall it. Document files in cloud storage take up little room. Following is an example of how you can organize your files, and I'll expand one section so you get the idea.

- College Life/Misc.
- Science
- Math
- History
  - American History 101
  - American History 102
  - Western Civilization 201
    - Syllabus/Misc.
    - Lecture Notes
      - Unit 1
      - Unit 2
      - Unit 3
    - Quizzes
      - Prep
      - Graded
    - Tests
      - Study Guides
      - Graded
    - Research Paper
      - Requirements
      - Ideas/Outline
      - Sources
      - Manuscript
  - Western Civilization 202

- English
- Foreign Language
- Major
- Electives
- Networking
- Volunteer
- Personal

It takes only seconds to create these folders as you're saving your work.

Again, take the time to watch a tutorial or short video on tips and tricks for whatever technology you're using, to save you time and allow you to get the most out of the product. Many a student has lost a letter grade because they failed to learn the software that should have helped them. Learn how to set margins, insert data, or change the spacing before you start writing.

Let's back up now and get our idea and thesis together. You may not have a say on the subject because your professor assigns a specific topic and a clear direction. Either way, following are some ways to develop ideas for your subject. Whether through an internet search or the library's search engines, find out what others have written about the topic. For example, you can run a search for "leading philosophers on free will." You can search in question format: "Why did Lincoln choose Ulysses Grant to lead the Union Army?" Or state it simply: "research sources on the laws of motion." Not only are you searching for sources, but you're looking for angles, a direction, and paragraph builders.

With any luck, you'll probably find other research papers on similar subjects. Take the time to see how they're structured. How did they set up the introduction? Did they develop their thesis? Does the formatting look correct? A word of caution, and let me state this as emphatically as I can—do not plagiarize! Never, ever use someone else's work without a clear citation. Using their rough idea or a brief paraphrase may not require quotation marks, but even that requires a citation such as a footnote, endnote, or in-text. It's always wrong, and it can get you kicked out of school. Consider another paper written on your topic a potential model that can help you work out your idea. You might even remember a portion of a paper you've previously written that helps birth a new idea.

The most common type of paper you've probably written, and likely mastered for the SAT, is the five-paragraph essay. If you're not familiar with it, or need a refresher, the first paragraph is an introduction, telling the reader the thesis and how you'll support it. The next three paragraphs each cover one supporting point. The fifth paragraph is the conclusion, summarizing why the reader should care or be convinced. All your research papers can work from this same structure, regardless of size. I'll admit that a technical paper or experiment write-up may look a little different, but the same principle applies. Let me show you an example.

Your government class requires a six-page paper and you've chosen "the pros and cons of term limits" as your topic. The structure of the five-paragraph paper works here because you'll have an introduction that might be two paragraphs, several supporting paragraphs, and a concluding paragraph. The intro is longer because you have more points to introduce. You'll state your thesis—the question you seek to answer or why something is true—and then give a roadmap for how you'll do that. Keep the conclusion concise because a strong paper has already convinced the reader. You might connect it to one of your opening statements, but the conclusion simply draws the paper to a close.

Now for the meaty middle. The intro and conclusion will probably take up one page, so how do you build the other five? You need to outline. Some can write by the seat of their pants with no planning (these people are called pantsters in writing circles), but most of us cannot. We need a map (we're called plotters). The outline gets us there. Here's a sample:

I. Introduction
   A. Thesis statement
   B. Supporting direction

II. The history of term limits
   A. Athens, Rome
   B. Modern
   C. By type of office
III. Arguments against term limits
   A. Experience
   B. Devoted service
   C. Less campaigning
IV. Arguments for term limits
   A. New perspectives
   B. Money
   C. Breakup Old Boys' Club
      1. Corruption
         a) By individual
            (1) Example from 1960 election
            (2) Example from 2018 election
         b) Local election leader
         c) By party officials
         d) Cronyism
      2. One party maintains power longer
      3. Gerrymandering
V. Conclusion

For the example, I didn't develop every section as I did for IV. C., but you can see how it can be done. It's like a snowball rolling downhill and picking up new pieces. Let's see how this outline may translate into the contents of your paper. Though it'll be longer, your six-page paper can still be structured like a five-paragraph essay. You won't have a one-paragraph introduction where you tell the reader the points you'll make per each of the following three paragraphs, but you can use two introductory paragraphs, perhaps, to explain the overall ideas behind enacting or not enacting term limits (which you will still expand upon in the coming paragraphs). Every other outline point will become a sentence, a few sentences, or a whole paragraph. Remember one of the first things I talked about in this book? Small bites. You're drafting your paper in small bites that all correlate to a larger work.

If you can, write your paper over several weeks. This gives you time to think about ways to tweak sentences or develop sections. "Is that harder and will it interrupt my flow of thought?" you might ask yourself. It might, so you may need to write the paper in one sitting or over a couple of days. But only consider doing this if you've completed the research phase, created the outline, documented your resources, and crafted some powerful sentences to open with. If so, make sure you complete that first draft at least one week before it's due. Write it and leave it for a day or so. Then, come back, refreshed, and ready to polish for content and clarity. William Strunk Jr. and E.B. White wrote a handy guide called *The Elements of Style* with tons of writing tips you can use to polish your work.

When should you begin taking notes? As soon as you've identified the topic and thesis, begin the note-taking process. It's never too early to jot down facts, ideas, and source locations. Use that note-taking app, voice recorder, or good ol' pen and paper. Ideally, you'll have a rough outline written and you can write your notes and location of sources there. I'll typically keep a notepad nearby or a sticky note in a book I'm referencing and jot down page numbers with one word that ties those pages to an outline point. If reading with a pen, it'll be a quick process to jot that note and jump right back to reading. Notes can be about anything, and you may not use all of them. They might be a reminder to look for a certain article, the location of a quote, or a sentence that comes to you that you want to use in a paper.

I like to footnote and build my bibliography or works cited page as I write. I realize for some this may break their flow of thought. That's fine, but make sure you leave time for that, know exactly what needs notation, and know how to create the list. I use a cloud-based software called EasyBib that finds the book and cites according to the citation method I'm using. It's a great way to collect my sources. In the end, it's simple copy-and-paste. The footnotes in this book and bibliography at the end are a product of that. If you have any doubts about how to create your bibliography, practice citing a few sources you know you'll use before you begin; that way, there are no surprises. The bibliography is completed days before your paper is due, not the night before.

What happens if you get stuck while writing? The dreaded writer's block as they say. Here are a few tactics. Start with a quote from one of your sources. Then, try to develop a couple of sentences that can go before and after the quote to see if that helps stir up some direction. Another idea is to skip to the last sentence you planned to write in the paragraph and work backward. If the block persists, you might just need to skip to the next section of your paper. If needed, stand up and splash water on your face or do jumping jacks. Come back, thumb through your resources and notes, and take another look. Whatever you do, don't give up or start some time-wasting activity. Treat this like a job. This is the time you devoted to writing. Don't loaf on the job.

A quick paragraph on essay exams or papers that must be written during a class test. Let's assume you're given a few potential topics, then the best way to prepare is to write out outlines for each topic. The chapter on memory is a huge help here. I'd also suggest having memorized three or four quotes from well-known persons that can color your essay. Quotes are easy enough to find, but make sure you put them in quotation marks and use appropriate attribution.

Because you've read intently and efficiently, you've used your research time diligently, you have a thorough outline, and your outline has a ton of notes, the actual writing of the long form research paper is simply the next step in the process. For some, it might be the easiest step. Remember, you've already ensured you know how to format, whether endnotes or footnotes are required, and how many sources you need. Mastering college means planning ahead. It's easier and less stressful.

A quick word on typing skills. Students once took an archaic class called Typing. We sat in front of typewriters and banged away earning a strong 35 WPM to satisfy our teacher. As the average family came to have more than one computer, students took keyboarding, but now, most grow up on a keyboard and develop their typing skills, almost, naturally. Maybe that's not you. There are loads of typing courses online that can be done in minutes a day to speed up your typing so your fingers can match the pace of your mind as you craft those brilliant research papers. Don't let poor typing skills bog you down. Develop your typing so you can regularly produce 50 to 60 WPM or so.

Recommended Reading: Strunk, William, and E. B. White. *The Elements of Style*. New York: Macmillan, 1972.

8.

SYNCHRONIZING MIND AND BODY

Do you understand how to exercise your brain? Much like a muscle after a strong workout routine that grows and makes your body healthier, your brain creates new dendrites whenever you process new information through listening, talking, writing, and practice. The more dendrites, the easier your synapses fire neurotransmitters. The more frequent the activity, as in daily, for example, the faster dendrites grow. So much of your college activity does this to your brain without you even realizing it's happening.

That's the gift of that foreign language class. While some majors don't have this requirement, many require four semesters of study in one language. There are plenty of reasons to value this subject, from opening doors in your career to expanding your reading comprehension.

Learning French, for example, will give you a greater capacity for your English vocabulary due to greater knowledge of cognates or common roots that build words. Knowing Spanish is great for a career in the Southwest. Imagine helping someone in need that doesn't speak English. Businesses are finding the knowledge of Mandarin a valuable skill. Wouldn't it be fun to converse in Italian on that dream vacation? So, you can see both the practical and the unseen value of that Intermediate German class. We can make a case for any course, but fortunately, you typically have a choice in the language you study.

How do you balance all that brain activity and the constant pressure of assignments for a healthy college lifestyle? You need to take breaks. If needed, schedule them. Much of what you've read so far will, hopefully, when applied, keep your stress level near to nonexistent. That's one of my main goals in teaching you these concepts. Let's say you have no stress but always feel as though you can study a little more. I can't tell you when to stop. But you need to take breaks throughout the day for your mind and your body. Louis Pasteur said that "Chance favors only the prepared mind." That doesn't always mean a mind packed with information. It means one that's rested as well.

Many students fall in the trap of spending more time on breaks than on their studies. You have the best intentions. You plan a quick check of your social media newsfeed, and 90 minutes later, you realize you wasted valuable study time and are now late for class. Don't be that person. Or maybe you've studied for over an hour and need to leave for class immediately. Study first, plan a fifteen-minute social media break, and then go to class. That way there's no wasted time and no guilt. Maybe you want to watch some streaming media on your phone while you eat lunch. Go for it. But set a timer on your phone and have the discipline to not click on that next episode.

Breaks are awesome. They recharge us. Motivate us. But they can also trap us. Beware! Think of your break as an apple pie. You wouldn't eat the whole pie in one sitting. Plan for one slice at a time. Hopefully, you'll get so efficient at your studies, you can easily take one or two days off a week. As in, the whole day to relax. It's good to work, but it's also great to relax.

Let's switch to your physical health for a moment. At this point, you may be thinking that I'm suggesting you plan every minute of your life, 24/7. I'm not. If you want to do that, feel free, but don't over schedule your life. I've never put "sleep" on my calendar. However, I know I need at least seven hours for optimal performance and can function with six. I give that only a few seconds thought in the late evening in relation to the time I need to wake in the morning. Don't skimp on sleep. Try to keep a routine. Even if you have classes starting at 8:30 on Mondays and Wednesdays but 11:00 on Tuesdays and Thursdays, plan to wake at the same time each day. Our bodies respond better to these circadian rhythms. If you've ever taken an overseas trip and experienced jet lag, you understand the importance of steady sleep patterns.

Are you a workout nut? Then you probably don't need any motivation to exercise on a regular basis. You may already have cardio days and strength day. Maybe even leg day. At a minimum, spending twenty-five to thirty minutes on cardiovascular activity three to five days per week is heart healthy, and you'll feel better. It's a great time to enjoy music, podcasts, or audiobooks. Maybe you're struggling to understand hydrogen bonds for that chemistry class. I guarantee you can find a podcast discussing it. Fifteen minutes on the treadmill or walking around campus while reinforcing that topic followed by ten minutes of your favorite music is time well spent.

Does the thought of exercise make you cringe? You don't have to wear workout clothes and use a machine. Walking is a viable option. I like to walk on the treadmill and watch movies. I try to stop just as something interesting is about to happen in the film. It motivates me to get back on that treadmill. What motivates you? Don't get hung up on the method. Develop the habit. It's good for you. Over time, you may need that little push that comes from an exercise class. Work your way up slowly. You don't need to start with a marathon. Small bites—or steps—in this case.

Intramural sports are a great option. Most colleges have all sorts of organized sports available, such as basketball, soccer, or tennis. They have leagues and seasons just like the main programs. It's a great way to challenge yourself, get some exercise, and make friends.

Another element affects both mind and body—your spiritual health. I have no intent to change or make any assumption about your beliefs, so please don't tune out. I realize that "spirituality" can carry a heavy connotation. At a minimum, realize that deep within you are needs not always solved with a physical solution or mental drill. Consider that need for joy, wonder, happiness, empathy, goodness, love, and peace.

For those of a regular faith, it's not always easy to find those same spiritual disciplines you had while at home. You likely attended church with your parents and joined your friends for some fellowship event or service project. Maybe you started your day reading Scripture or in prayer. Why should that change when you're at college? I can hear the reasons, but for every reason, will that be your reason when you've graduated and are living on your own?

If this is you, I strongly encourage you to make three things a priority. One, set a regular time every day for prayer and Scripture reading. Maybe it's in the morning, at lunch, or before your head hits the pillow. Two, find a local church where you can worship with others of similar faith. It's okay to try a few different ones until you feel at home. Three, join others on campus that share your passion for service, community projects, or outreach. Almost every campus has a group that brings students of that faith together for fellowship, spiritual study, and service.

Maybe religion has no place in your life. Ask yourself where you can turn when you're stressed, had a bad day, need some encouragement, or want to share a success. Call home. Don't ever think of that as a weakness. Your parents are thinking about you. They're wondering how your day went. How you did on that test. Whether you're eating and sleeping. Trust me. I'm a parent with college-aged children. I know it's true. Calling them from time to time will give them peace, but it also provides you that nourishment of assurance you need.

What do you do if you feel things are slipping? Number one, don't panic. Number two, don't wait or avoid the problem. Tell someone. Maybe it's a pastor, priest, or rabbi. Your parents. A friend. Your roommate. If needed, go see your advisor. Share your struggles and ask them for advice. Holding in negative feelings can make your problems worse. Finding that person who can be your sounding board is a vital step in your spiritual and emotional health. It's not a weakness. It's a perfectly healthy thing to do.

I could write a whole book on keeping a positive attitude, but many have already done that. Most of them will stress that you have to focus on the truth. "My professor wants me to fail." True? Of course not. "There's no way I'll ever get through college." True? Most do get through college. Stay focused on the truth that you know how to devise a plan, follow it, and finish your work. You've got this.

The typical semester lasts sixteen weeks. The first couple of weeks you're catching your breath. The next several weeks you're settling into a routine. Midterms offer time to put a heavy load behind you. A break is hopefully scheduled to give you a few days off. Then, you're back in that routine with finals looming. I was the type of student that never felt like I could relax until the semester finished. I felt I could always study a little more, read ahead, or tweak that paper. In hindsight, I wish I had adjusted my attitude and recognized these little periods of completeness. I didn't appreciate finishing small bites. I want more for you. I want you to take those small bites, do them with excellence, take a short break, and attack the next one.

There's a time for work and a time to play. You can have a healthy dose of both. If you begin to wonder about that balance, that is, whether you're allowing too much work or too much play, here's what you can do. Cut back on ten percent of the one that you think is too much. After a week or so, how does it feel? If you cut back on ten percent of your play time, are you any less unhappy or unfulfilled? Or, are you glad you had that extra time to finish a paper? If you're feeling like a workaholic, trim off ten percent of your study time for a week or so. Did your grades suffer? Regardless of which one, keep tweaking that calendar until you get the proper balance of mind, body—and spirit.

9.

A BEAUTIFUL MIND WAS RIGHT ABOUT TEAMWORK

The 2001 film *A Beautiful Mind* tells the story of John Forbes Nash Jr., a brilliant mathematician that suffered from schizophrenia. Within that tragic tale is revealed the theorem for which he won the Nobel Prize for economics. His work on strategy and competition explains how individuals benefit from working for themselves as well as for the group as a whole. As a student, you're likely concerned about your own grade, but what if you were as equally passionate about the grades of others?

College courses, by their nature, are not created for competition. There's no benefit to anyone failing and only upside for everyone doing well. I'm not referring to academic competitions or scholarships. There's absolutely competition here and there. I'm referring to the average courses that make up the bulk of your college life. Following are several examples of how you can work out Nash's theory, but most importantly, why a synergistic mindset for teamwork is vital.

I found there are four types of members to a team: doers, drainers, drivers, and dreamers. The doer makes things happen and keeps the flow. They're the ones that don't argue with the method and finish their portion on time. We need doers. The drainer has the opposite effect on production. They complain about the assignment and make excuses for not doing their share. We don't need them. The driver leads the team. They get things organized and make sure everyone participates. We must have drivers. The dreamer has that creative idea or epiphany. We love having a dreamer on the team. Which one are you?

Study groups are the most obvious way to build a team approach to a class. Law school students find them invaluable for discussion of a previous lecture or major legal concepts. They're easy to start. Just find a few friends or classmates and agree to meet on a regular basis. If the group is too small, you'll lose the value of multiple minds, but two people can get it done. Too large a group and chaos can cause inefficiency.

Three to five works well. The organizer, typically a driver-type, sets the expectations. Be on time. Be prepared. Be beneficial. The first two are common courtesy. Drainers typically violate those things. Being beneficial doesn't mean you've mastered the class. It might mean quite the opposite. You might be the one needing the most help. That's okay. That's part of the group's mission. A willingness to listen and learn goes a long way because someone else in the study group may be there to help you. By explaining concepts to you, they strengthen their grasp of the course. It's a win-win. It's synergy.

Don't think of a study group as a shortcut to completing your homework. A study partner might offer a tip if you're stuck, but you must still do the work. Think of the group more as a venue to discuss concepts, develop approaches to major assignments, bounce research topic ideas off one another, share outlines, and study for a major exam. In a nutshell, study groups are more topic or course driven. You could form a group in high school or college to discuss the principles in this book, one chapter per meeting.

Study partners are more about accountability. Imagine if you found one person equally passionate about mastering college and you shared your academic calendar with them? You might not sit together and study every day, but you might communicate once or twice a day with a word of encouragement or reminder to stick to the plan. Does that sound cheesy? Who cares? You're tackling college with a plan. You're mastering it.

A critique group of two or more students does just that—critique one another's work, such as research papers. The word "critique" sounds harsh, but it really just means evaluate. Let's say you have a group made up of three people that all have research papers due at about the same time. The first meeting might be a brainstorming session with a plan to create outlines and have the first page written by the next meeting. At that next meeting, you can take turns reading another person's work aloud. Don't read your own. It's better for you to hear it read. Here, you're critiquing for clarity and persuasion. Depending on the size of the project, that step might continue over the next few weeks. A final meeting might be trading papers and proofreading for typos and formatting. An important note: You should ask your professor's permission for this level of cooperation, particularly if your papers are on closely related subjects.

Group projects, especially senior projects, need special attention. You may even want to use free cloud-based software for team or project management so you can share documents, to-do lists, communications, and progress. Some software usually has a short learning curve, but it's worth the time. There are so many options I hesitate to recommend one over another. Something as simple as a shared calendar can even work. It seems awfully official, but setting expectations and assignments in writing, and having members sign off on their role, may make for a more committed team. Putting one's name on a pledge has the power of creating accountability.

Clubs are great for taking your studies further and rounding out things you might be missing. Members are passionate about the subject and desire to help. Are you struggling with that French class? The French club will offer tutoring and exposure to French culture. Your professor may even give you extra credit for joining. Do some concepts in biology seem confusing? Visit the biology club and ask them for some club activities based on that concept. If you're tone deaf and struggle with music, do you give up? Nope. You find some musicians and hang out with them. You may see your professor sitting next to you. Show them you care about the subject they've devoted their lives to.

Earlier in this book, I told you to think like a professor. Now I'm asking you to think like a roommate. A good roommate keeps to themselves, cleans after themselves, and holds the distractions to a minimum. There's nothing wrong with that. A great roommate partners with you in this college adventure. They can be there for accountability, study, and critique. There may be no greater teammate for you during this time of your life. What kind of roommate do you want? Be that person.

10.

TO GREEK OR NOT TO GREEK

The social organizations we call fraternities and sororities have a long history and make up what's known as the Greek system because each house is named after two or three letters of the Greek alphabet. (In this chapter, I'll refer only to fraternities, but know that in each instance, the same could apply to sororities.) You'll find plenty of members praising their membership, but these organizations can also have some negative consequences.

I'm not anti-Greek, but I am Greek-cautious. I don't see these as a necessity but look at them like any other group or activity you can join to enhance your college experience. I'll offer a few advantages and disadvantages to joining one of these organizations, but I encourage you to do your own investigation into a particular fraternity and, specifically, how it's run at the school you're attending. Find alumni and have a list of questions ready.

If Hollywood were your only guide, you'd think the Greek life of fraternity membership makes up the majority of your college experience. While some films focus on that, it's not the actual college experience for many. The most important question you must ask is, why do you want to join one? Is it for social reasons? Do you think it will help you academically? Partying? Why are you going to college?

First some advantages. Most fraternities make it difficult to join.

That alone offers an elite status that you desire and can open doors for you in college and later in life. The networking options are tremendous. Many businesspeople today partner together based on their shared Greek status. Fraternities participate in philanthropic and charitable activities that serve the needy. Most members look back on their fraternity days as some of their most enjoyable and, from them, have gained lifelong friends. They loved communal living under one roof. Many of their activities gave them great teamwork and leadership experience.

There are disadvantages. A fraternity can drain the bank with endless expenses: apparel, dues, or the push to match the lifestyle of other members. It can also drain your time, as members are required to participate in fraternity activities. Some fraternities overemphasize the partying aspect of college life without much concern for academics. A few of these groups may frown upon you associating with non-members or carry a feeling of superiority. It could cause you to lose existing friends.

The greatest downside of fraternities is hazing, an act illegal in most states and against most school policies. Is there a positive aspect of hazing? I've never heard of one. Some suggest it encourages teamwork as pledges band together in their time of trial. I get that, but I can think of plenty of alternatives that don't involve bullying, degradation, illegal acts, branding, nudity, corporal punishment, and alcohol.

I don't argue with a barrier to entry or rite of passage, but here are a few tests to find out if the ritual is appropriate. Does the school find it acceptable and is it comfortable with the general public witnessing the event? Are both parties laughing? If only the tormentor is laughing, it's probably bullying. If someone receives a permanent injury, it's downright dangerous. If it's illegal, no further discussion necessary. If it must be done in secret, that's a red flag or at least a cause for concern.

Smart fraternities organize team-building activities that pit their pledges against another fraternity's pledges. It's all good, clean, fun as they say. Some pledging might require hard and taxing work, showing a willingness to devote that kind of hard work when the entire group does a civic project. Don't let anyone do anything to abuse you. Do you really want to join an organization that does that anyway?

Secret societies have a long tradition, such as Skull and Bones at Yale. While it may be difficult for you to fully investigate an organization like that when asked to join, I'd encourage you to proceed with caution and be willing to bow out if they suggest you do something against your standards.

Don't let hazing or the willingness of some in other chapters to break the rules keep you from joining a fraternity. There's plenty of hazing in other organizations, such as the military, public school, professional sports teams, and even workplaces. It should be against those organization's rules or policies. Keep your confidence. Maintain your power and dignity. Own your college experience.

Let's look a little more closely at some alternatives to going all Greek. We've already mentioned joining a particular club to help you with certain academic subjects, and larger schools have clubs for nearly anything you can imagine. If they don't, there's always the option of starting one. Membership to certain academic clubs requires a high GPA in the area of study. Most clubs require a smaller time commitment than fraternities and an opportunity to take a semester off if necessary. Beware of overcommitting. Sometimes giving up that Tuesday night commitment is all that's needed to right the ship, academically speaking.

For those that like politics, participation in student government may offer great networking. Maybe you just want something fun to do. Some schools have *Harry Potter* clubs. Theatre, religion, journalism, and similar clubs can fill the void, and you'll likely find great friends. Clubs are great resume builders too. Conversely, their absence on a resume might concern a future employer. That statement alone suggests you should try a few. Especially those that serve the less fortunate.

We've talked about thinking like a professor and thinking like a roommate. Now think like someone in need. If you're following the principles of this book, not only will you have more free time to relax, but you'll have time to give back to the community or to society. A lot of clubs link to or may even be devoted to a charitable cause. Your activity in this area will reward you and tangibly help someone. Imagine helping to build a house for a needy family or traveling to South America to teach orphans.

Nearly all fraternities and clubs can build discipline, teamwork, and leadership traits. They look great on a resume. You'll gain confidence, camaraderie, and a sense of achievement. Some might lead to a connection, internship, or job. Part of the college experience is rounding out your portfolio. Whether you join that fraternity or club, make sure it's healthy for your mind and body and never interferes with academics.

11.

THE MATH LAB IS YOUR FRIEND

Two trains are traveling in opposite directions. One is heading south at 45 miles per hour. The other is heading north at 51 miles per hour. A bird is riding on the southbound train and weighs 0.5 pounds while a rabbit is on the northbound train and weighs 3.0 pounds. As they pass, the bird flies toward the rabbit with velocity of…Okay, I made up that ridiculous word problem. Do those types of math problems cause you consternation? Maybe for you, it's applying the quadratic formula or simply any problem that includes an "x." If you excel at math or have no fears of calculus, don't tune out. There's still plenty in this chapter to make you more efficient with math, and these concepts can help with virtually any course.

For those with math struggles, I feel your pain, but I also have a plan for you. First, though, some background.

I once met someone that quit college after completing 117 credit hours. She lacked one class required for her degree—College Algebra. The subject paralyzed her. She passed algebra in her sophomore year of high school but had procrastinated taking college-level algebra until her last college semester. Lost a few weeks in, she dropped the class and never graduated. She wasn't the only one. I've met others who pushed courses like that to the tail end of their degree and then lacked the fortitude to tackle them and simply dropped out of college.

I never did well in math and hated word problems. So many times, I uttered the common phrase, "I'll never need this." I was wrong, of course, because I've used math my whole life. Not every unit from every textbook, but the concepts, critical thinking skills, the building of dendrites, and practical problem-solving methods benefit me to this day. They will benefit you as well. As with every course you take, know that math builds your overall knowledge base.

I joined the U.S. Navy and left for boot camp just nine days after my high school graduation. When I decided to attend college a couple of years after discharge, the school required I take an assessment exam. I did okay on the writing/reading portion, but they placed me in remedial math. Not just for one semester, but two. I had to complete both elementary algebra and intermediate algebra before taking the credit course of college algebra. The last math class I had taken had been a high school course in the tenth grade. So, though I had used plenty of math in those eight years, I had not added exponents or considered the formula for finding the slope.

For many, math can be similar to a foreign language in that the intricacies or building blocks you learn, if not used over time, can be lost. For that reason, I strongly urge you to take any required math courses in your first two semesters. Technical majors like engineers will take several semesters of math in their first years because they need those foundations as they work in other science courses. Most non-technical degrees require only six credit hours, so why not put them behind you in your first year? If you're a liberal arts major, for example, you can find alternative math courses that are more interesting to you or better align with your major. Philosophy of logic is one example, and some colleges offer a course literally called Math for Liberal Arts Majors.

After I finished those two remedial courses, I decided to pursue an engineering degree. One class built upon another until I had taken and passed College Algebra, Trigonometry, Calculus I, Calculus II, Calculus III, Analytical Geometry, and Differential Equations. I don't list those to impress you. I list them to explain that I was, and am, an average math student. Two fundamental principles which I'm about to cover gave me the tools to work through all of them. So, the time it takes to read this chapter will save you hours of frustration and remove the barrier of that dreaded math course.

My professor for an accounting course opened the first class by stating that accounting is not a math course. It's a language course. She urged us to learn the language of accounting and then the numbers would work themselves out. Similarly, think of algebra, for example, as one of math's languages. That's the first principle. Once you grasp some basic translations, the numbers will fall in place. Here's a simple example.

What is 10% of 100? Easy, right? The answer is 10, but let's convert that plain-English sentence into algebra. The word "what" is the unknown represented by "x." The word "is" means equal. Percentage converts to hundredths, so slide that decimal point two digits over. That 10 is really 10.0, but we have it rounded in the sentence. So, expressing 10 as a percentage is 0.10. What about "of"? That's our multiplication word represented by a vertically centered dot.

The Problem: What is 10% of 100?
    Converted: $x = 0.10 \cdot 100$
    Solution: $x = 10$

You may not even understand how to convert the percentage, but I hope you see the concept of translation between math and English. Here's another example, in reverse.

The Problem: $x - 6 = 2$
    Converted: What subtracted by six is two?
    Solution: 8

"Pure mathematics is, in its way, the poetry of logical ideas," according to Albert Einstein. The more connections you make between your fluent language (English), the more you'll understand mathematical language. We can make these same comparisons for geometry, finite mathematics, or other math courses. My Calculus II professor had worked as an engineer. One day he drew a bridge on the board and explained how engineers had to calculate a structural element. The unit we learned that day solved that problem. That brilliant teacher gave us those real-world examples often. However, you're not always given a real-world example. Don't get bogged down by contemplating the practical application of every problem. Trust that you're building toward something greater. Math, like many courses, requires the learning of building blocks. Small bites, that is.

Now for the second principle: tutoring. I had an army of willing participants that helped me along the way. Before you scoff, when I say tutor, I'm not talking about a bespectacled taskmaster standing over me with a ruler. Mainly, I found tutors for free in the math lab. Nearly every college has space where paid or volunteer tutors will help you. If you don't have a dedicated math lab, there are alternatives, such as your professor, their graduate assistant, the math department, a paid tutor, or a volunteer willing to help. A math major working toward a teaching degree should jump at the chance to help you. In addition, you'll find hundreds of videos online for every math concept. Finding a tutor is rarely an issue. Read the following with the assumption that you'll likely have a math lab at your disposal.

Unlike some courses where you can skip a few days while preparing for a specific research paper or test, math is a daily process, save perhaps for one or two days off during the course of a week. You must do all the homework prior to the next class. Moreover, you must understand every problem from the lecture and your homework before you walk into that next math class. That's the big secret to my success. If I left a class baffled or confused on a fundamental point, I went to the math lab where they helped me reach a level of understanding from which I could tackle the homework problems. Then, I finished the homework by the next day. If I still needed help, I left early and was back in the math lab before class.

If, after a lecture, I left feeling only slightly confused on a problem or two, or highly confident, I skipped the lab and made sure my homework was completely done by the next day. If I didn't understand something—even one problem on the homework—I left for school early and went to the math lab first. Every time I returned for the next math lecture, I had understood and completed 100% of the homework. I learned this process during that first elementary algebra course when the professor mentioned the math lab. I was so frustrated by not grasping simple concepts the rest of the class seemed to understand. I was five years older than most of them and tried to use that as an excuse. The math tutors helped me work through the issue, gave me some test strategies, and I made an "A" on my very first college exam. It was a proud moment for me and the day I decided I'd never settle for anything less than excellence in my schoolwork. I went on to make an "A" in the course.

And so it went. Lecture, homework, lab, back to lecture. Repeat. I'm not saying it was easy, but I know it made those courses more efficient. Rather than hours of homework frustration, I flew through my math homework because I understood how to do most of the problems if not all of them. If I got stumped on one or two, I put in the time to think through and figure them out. I never crumpled paper or threw my hands in the air. I gave it an honest try and, if unsuccessful, put it aside for my tutor. Smarter, not harder. Math made easy.

12.

SHEEP AND WOLVES

Not every opponent is a wolf, and I'm not necessarily calling you a sheep, but it's important you learn to separate the two. We'll consider the broad spectrum of those you'll face, from the friendly opponent to the criminal. You need to think like them so you're prepared for those challenges when—not if—they come. We don't want to live so cynically that we assume everyone's out to get us. We want to walk and talk with confidence and stand our ground.

I've already introduced the concept of thinking like a professor and more, but now I want you to think like an opponent. It's done all the time in sports, chess, and political debate. In *To Kill a Mockingbird*, Atticus Finch counsels his daughter Scout by saying, "You never really understand a person until you consider things from his point of view…until you climb into his skin and walk around in it."[2] He's teaching Scout how she can better relate to others. This pearl of wisdom can give you an easier path to avoid unneeded conflict and reduce frustration. However, sometimes conflict lands at your doorstep. Are you ready?

I'm a huge believer that the truth will always win out. It's hard to watch someone lie or cheat their way to gaining an advantage. You

---

[2] Harper Lee, *To Kill a Mockingbird* (New York: Scribner Laidlaw, 1989), 33.

may be tempted to utter a silent prayer that the cosmos will exact some karma-like revenge on them. Don't find complacency in that. Know the truth, and stick to it. That's the long game that will ultimately win. I love this quote attributed to St. Augustine, "The truth is like a lion; you don't have to defend it. Let it loose; it will defend itself."

I strongly recommend studying the logical fallacies people typically use. Learn how to recognize them and why they weaken an opponent's stance. I can spot two to three every hour on cable news. Here are a few examples of logical fallacies you've probably heard of. A red herring is where someone strays from the argument with a point that's related but which avoids them dealing with the real argument at hand. You might see this if a reporter presses a politician on his position regarding the death penalty but the politician cites an unrelated statistic. The ad hominem occurs when someone attacks the person rather than the argument. "Sarah is a bigot, so I don't believe her when she says she wants to help the homeless." Another is the part-to-whole fallacy, where the user suggests that what happens with a small sample of a group will or has happened to the whole group. An example might be when someone says a certain car model is a lemon; therefore, all cars by that maker are lemons.

By studying and identifying logical fallacies, you'll find you can quickly dispense with their poor argument and make your point, one that follows logic and truth. *The Fallacy Detective* is an excellent resource. Don't let the cover fool you. All ages, from children to adults, can learn and use this teaching. I'm not suggesting you go looking for an argument just as I wouldn't tell you to go looking for a fight. I'm suggesting preparation for situations that may arise in the dorm, in the cafe, or in the classroom. The goal is not so much to win but rather to stand your ground.

Is the professor always right? What happens if a professor makes a statement that you know is untrue, antithetical to science, insulting to your religion, or simply reflects a politically partisan view? I can't give you a definitive answer on when you should throw your hand up and challenge your professor. I once had a government teacher that told us up front his political persuasion but invited us to debate with him, respectfully, so we could not only weigh the issues but push ourselves to learn the extremes of both sides. He argued against the death penalty while some students argued for it. He pushed each side to present valid support for our stance. We gained so much by this. However, I heard a story where a professor noticed an engagement ring on a student and chastised her for wanting to be married, as if marriage contradicted her feminism. Professors are human, too. Most are passionate about teaching you, but prepare yourself when they forget their place.

If the debate is invitational, engage but don't take over the room. Make your point and allow others to chime in. When they make their points, look them in the eye so they know you're listening. Avoid interrupting, raising your voice, or talking over others. Your opponent may do that to you and seemingly "win," but like telling the truth, cooler heads typically prevail. If you sense a professor is not welcoming debate, keep your hand down and hold your tongue. The professor has the authority in the classroom, not you. Visit them during office hours. They'll probably be more open to your side of an issue in the privacy of their office than if you challenge them openly in the classroom. More than once I've heard a professor correct themselves for something they said in a previous lecture.

Another option is saving your thoughts for your study group, parents, or friends. Work out your argument with them first to make sure you're on the right track. We live in an age where political views are polarizing, and many don't understand the differences between hypothetical, theoretical, and empirical science. We fear another's religion or simply forget Atticus Finch's teaching to see things from their point of view. Winning hearts and minds doesn't mean you have to agree with the other person. Showing value in their opinion and letting others be heard goes a long way. Resist the urge to win every argument. Focus, rather, on obtaining a commanding view of both sides of any argument. Stephen Prothero authored a book called *Religious Literacy: What Every American Needs to Know—and Doesn't* with that point in mind. He didn't push one religion over another but knew that education on why people believe what they believe made for a more informed society.

I'd love to say that your college experience will be conflict-free and that your days of facing verbal abuse or bullying ended when you left high school. The sad fact is that immature, selfish, judgmental, and oppressive people exist in college, and you will encounter them for the rest of your life. As I said in the first chapter, many of the things I'm teaching you not only apply to college but will work for you in life. As we become adults, bullying becomes more verbal than physical, but there are ways to prepare for both.

We typically think of two roles in a bullying situation: the bully and the victim. I can only make a few suggestions on how to avoid targeting by a bully. It may seem unfair, but when you spot them, avoid their lair. Take a different route. Don't make eye contact. If they engage you with a verbal taunt, don't get into a tit-for-tat confrontation. Tell them, "I'm sorry. I really need to get to class," or even answer with, "I've got nothing." They want you to argue or fight back. Don't fall into their trap. If they seem determined to attack you for a particular reason, think of what you can do to keep that "reason" off their radar. If they say, "What are you looking at?" you can retort with, "Your shirt. I was wondering where you got it." Things like that can disarm them. Learning and practicing verbal self-defense can benefit you as much as the learning and practicing of physical self-defense.

What about fighting back? Wouldn't it be easier to strike back? Call them a name. Point out some flaw in their appearance. Punch them in the nose. I'm not telling you what you should do. I will urge you to not do anything illegal. All I can do is make suggestions about what you could do. Again, it's not fair, but you're focused on college, not on putting up with their foolishness.

There's typically a third party in these situations, and they sometimes have the most power. That's the bystander. Most bullies are committing their deed for what they think is the benefit of others. They hope to get a laugh from those watching. Nearly every bullying situation is defused when the bystander refuses to tolerate the spectacle. If you have that power, make your voice heard. Be the rescuer. You can literally grab the victim and escort them away, stating, "I'm sorry. We've got to go." What if there are three of you sitting together? The bully attacks the victim. You, the bystander, look at the bully and shake your head. Sometimes, that's all it takes.

I really don't want to tell you to think like a criminal; I'd rather have you consider what they typically do. Most colleges have adequate security measures for dangerous situations, and these will be explained to you during your orientation. These measures revolve around safety in the dorm, auto safety, walking from one building to another, moving around after dark, and dealing with inclement weather. Don't ignore these things. Add those emergency contacts to your phone and know where to go in a specific scenario.

It can take considerable time to develop solid self-defense techniques, but know that even beginners can learn enough to gain the advantage in a sticky situation. You should always seek out the authorities in the situations I discuss below, but I can introduce you to some techniques here. The main concept is to have situational awareness. This means staying alert to the potential for criminal or dangerous activity. Have you ever been in public and noticed someone that is acting strange or out of place? That doesn't make them a criminal, but it may be someone to keep your eye on. Or, you might just need to leave.

Gavin de Becker wrote *The Gift of Fear* where he suggests you trust your instincts. Sometimes something just doesn't feel right, and you can't explain it. It could be your other senses detecting subtle things. For example, you feel like someone is behind you, but you didn't hear anything. It might be your eyes caught a reflection in the window, or you felt the vibration of someone's footsteps. Don't neglect your gut instinct. It may be your actual, yet subtle, senses.

There's strength in numbers so travel in pairs or groups. Find someone in your late evening class that is headed your way. Many schools have escorts that will meet you and ensure you arrive safely to your car or dorm. This may seem inconvenient for you or them, but it's worth it. I once found myself in the college library basement all alone. I wasn't scared, but it didn't seem like a safe situation. I walked upstairs and returned later when a group of three went down to the basement. That was a combination of situational awareness, instinct, and practicality.

You may want to actively carry a certain type of weapon. I only suggest you make sure you meet legal guidelines as well as school policy. Make sure you know how that same weapon can be used against you. Don't carry any weapon unless you know how to keep it safe when not needed and how to use it when needed, you have practiced using it, and you can make sure it's always controlled by you.

One simple weapon I suggest everyone carry is a pen—commonly called a tactical defense pen. You can pay a lot of money for a military grade version, and they certainly work, but many times a steel-barreled pen that comes in a pack of two for a few dollars does the trick. A quick search on the internet will give you several tactics for using them. It's handier if the pen is in your front pocket or the lapel of a shirt. Imagine someone pinning you against a wall. With your free hand, you use the pen to repeatedly jab at the attacker. The pain you inflict on them will hopefully force them to release you and may give you those couple of seconds needed to run away. That cheaper steel pen, which is designed to be only a pen, is safe to carry, legal everywhere, and likely won't be used against you. A plastic pen can work but can easily break, so use the steel-barreled type.

What can you use as a weapon of opportunity? This is something that's already available in the location where you need to defend yourself. It might be something sharp (a butter knife) for stabbing or a club-shaped instrument (a broom) to poke the mid-section or strike the head. An aerosol can (bug spray) works like pepper spray. There are many others you can quickly make. Grab the nearest magazine, roll it up tight, and bang the end on your hand to make sure it's firm. A strike with that to the face of an attacker might do the trick, just as the corner of a laptop will knock someone back.

Most of us learned this technique when we were children: stop, drop, and roll if you're on fire. Similarly, federal government agencies such as the FBI and DHS teach basics that you can do in an active shooter situation. That is, to run, hide, fight. They don't necessarily mean all three. They mean for you to attempt each of those elements in order. If you can safely run away, get as far from the situation as possible. If you can't run, hide. If needed, fight back with all you've got, and use any weapon of opportunity. Work in groups. One strike low with a club to the kneecap and one stab high to the face with that rolled up magazine. I realize some of these things sound extreme, but I'd rather you over prepare.

Always seek the path of least resistance. What you do in those first few seconds can save you. Attempt a quick release, strike, yell, and run. I tell those I teach on self-defense to never go with an abductor, no matter the threat or weapon they're being threatened with; if they can, run. Personally, I'll take the chance of attempting to run away, because if I get in that car, for example, they're only going to take me someplace worse.

Should you take Brazilian jiu-jitsu or some other martial art? At a minimum, everyone should take a basic self-defense course. If you do take a martial art, you'll gain confidence and develop self-defense skills that will become second nature. That last part is what this whole chapter is about, learning mental, verbal, and physical skills that become second nature and which you'll remember in those few seconds when they're needed.

Recommended Reading: Bluedorn, Nathaniel, Hans Bluedorn, Rob Corley, and Tim Hodge. *The Fallacy Detective: Thirty-Eight Lessons on How to Recognize Bad Reasoning.* Quartz Hill, CA: Christian Logic, 2015.

De Becker, Gavin. *The Gift of Fear.* London: Bloomsbury, 2000.

13.

WE'RE HIRING

Should you or should you not work while in college? I'm not going to answer that question because only you can answer that. Though this chapter covers the topic of working while in college, I hope to offer so much more about how you might manage your time and your degree. That's the real goal of this chapter. Your college experience is an opportunity for you to practice your post-college life, where you'll be working in your career, living on your own, and paying your bills. How do you maximize your time to bring the most value to your degree?

It starts by taking ownership of your degree. Every required course, elective, club, job, and group you choose can benefit your degree. Should you have friends or do activities that don't feed into your degree plan? Absolutely, but from the day you begin working jobs or serving others, you're participating in things that can go on a future resume, and you have choices here. When you're forty years old, you probably won't list that fast food job, but when you graduate, you'll want to show that you held a steady job over time and can provide references. The same goes for volunteering at an orphanage in South America or leading a debate team. These things say something about you.

Since you own your degree, you should decide how to shape the final list of courses. Some degrees offer few electives, but others may allow near twenty-five percent of the course load to come from general subjects. A business major will find value in a history course on American industry. Journalism majors can take creative writing or screenwriting. I use skills that I learned in Introduction to Accounting to this day. Don't just take photography because you think it'll be easy. Take it because it will enhance your degree and you know you'll need that talent or base of knowledge in your career.

Foreign language study is one of the most underutilized electives. I explained why it's so helpful in the mind and body chapter. Most liberal arts degrees require fourteen hours in modern languages. That's four classes and two labs where you'll develop an intermediate level to hear, speak, read, and write the language. Most lose those skills because they stop using them. Regardless, they bring value because you learn so much about words in general, which helps you beyond knowing that certain language.

Graduate students will take one or two semesters of French, for example, focused solely on reading. By the end, they can read most French writing with little need for a dictionary and can correctly translate for their research. Now, what if you could do the same for learning to read Latin, Italian, or German? If you only read a little each day afterward, you'll keep that skill. Noting on your resume that you took four semesters of Spanish in college does not mean much, but if you can state that you "read Spanish fluently," prospective employers will take notice. This is how you need to build your degree. Ask yourself the following when considering an elective or club: Will I use it? Will it bring value to my resume? Will it enhance my major course of study?

Most curriculums are built something like this:

- 120 total hours of study
    - 60 hours of core courses that everyone at the university takes
        - 51 hours from required courses
        - 9 hours from free electives
    - 40 hours of required courses that are the same for those in that major
    - 20 hours of electives within that major field of study

Some schools require you to take certain core classes in the first and/or second year. Even if they don't, completing the core English courses early will give you a strong writing foundation, and chemistry or physics are needed for science majors. In fact, most of these are prerequisites and offer a great indicator of how well you've grasped a particular field. Those undecided on their major will want to take a variety of core courses to expose themselves to different fields. For example, introduction to psychology qualifies for most degrees' core curriculum, so you might take that to determine both your affinity and aptitude. Conversely, it may help you rule it out. Regardless, a foundation or basic introduction in certain non-required courses, such as philosophy, biology, sociology, theology, or the many other courses I've mentioned, brings value to any degree.

Now, addressing the question of whether you should work while you're in school is closely related to all we've discussed so far about owning your degree. For some of you, working while in school isn't even an option. You must work to pay your bills. If this is you, stay with me because I'll explain how you can maximize that in a bit. Some of you may want to work simply for the extra cash. Then, there are those of you who are fortunate enough to have finances covered and who can solely focus on school. Working might take time away from your studies. I'm going to suggest you work anyway. Research shows students that work ten to fifteen hours a week carry a higher GPA and some studies suggest a higher graduation rate.

There are a few reasons for this. Working students have less free time and thus have to be more diligent about planning their calendar. They say "no" to extra activities and develop a better work/study routine overall. These students also feel as if they're "working harder" for their degree and therefore treat their studies more seriously. Some of them find motivation from their current job—because they don't particularly love what they're doing, they're reminded how important their degree is. Others are working in a related field, and their job enhances what they're learning in the classroom. The same goes for military school cadets and student athletes. Like a job, those specialties require a large time commitment, forcing a full-time work mentality. For them, school is not made up of pockets during the week; rather, it entails a full week of duties similar to those of a nine-to-five schedule.

Can you avoid working a job and still excel with your coursework? Absolutely. Some can but many cannot. At a minimum, try working for one semester and measure your success. If you're convinced your academics are suffering, then take a break from working. Volunteering with an entity or participating in unpaid internships two or three times per week can mimic the benefits of working while in college, assuming it's a regular activity.

It goes without saying that if you can find work in a field similar to your degree, that's your best option. Local employers are always looking for help from those studying in the fields related to their business and will notify the school's career center of job openings. For example, a company that cares for the elderly would love nursing students to work as caregivers, and the students gain valuable experience by wearing scrubs and working with real patients. A small business may not need a full-time IT person but would love a computer science major to spend a couple of days per week making sure their computers are running smoothly. Maybe they need someone a little older to supervise their high school-aged help, and you'll gain valuable management experience.

What if you're working in retail, doing something completely unrelated to your degree? If you're a journalism major, ask them if you can update their website, write blog posts, or send out email campaigns. A film major could create a promotional video for the store that posts to social media. It might even double for a course project. Win-win. Think like an employer. For most of them, their most valuable asset is their people. They love when dedicated, young talent puts in a hard day's work for them. They especially love it when they know they're investing in your education. These are excellent resume builders, and your employer will most likely write you a nice reference letter.

With resources ranging from the school's career center and job boards to local advertising, there's really no excuse for not finding a job. Today's technology even gives you the opportunity to own your own business or franchise while in school. Driving, delivering, writing, editing, media creation, and call center support are only a few examples of work you can start on your own.

Write a professional resume and schedule as many interviews as you can. Run a search for sample interview questions and make a master list. Have an answer for at least thirty possible questions. Even the awkward "What are your weaknesses?" can be made positive. Here's an example answer. "I thrive on achievement, so I sometimes need to hone in on the two or three most important tasks of the day. Doing them well is the goal." If the first few don't hire you, don't be discouraged. Be thankful for the interview practice.

Inevitably, you'll be walking through the student center and see a table with some nice folks offering free T-shirts if you sign up for a credit card. Don't fall for it. Their goal, and how they make money, is ensuring you stay in debt. You didn't work so hard to find the right job, or to rent or buy used textbooks to save a hundred bucks, only to give the money to them after a shopping spree or dinner at a restaurant paid by the new credit card. Remember, college life is your practice for life after college. Staying out of debt alleviates stress and helps you focus on your school work.

An obvious and important benefit of working means you'll have cash coming in and gain experience with budgeting, saving, and giving. Zac Bissonnette's *Debt-Free U* has a ton of great ideas on how you can fund your college years and finish your degree with no debt. Imagine the head start you'll have in life without the burden of student loans. Imagine when you get that first paycheck after college and don't have a single debt payment.

Your school should offer a sample budget to help you plan. Some of you may have your tuition, books, fees, dorm, and food paid for, but others may need to include that in their budgets. You must find your school's sample for these costs since tuition varies greatly from one school to another. What else goes in your budget? Below I list some to think about, but make sure every regular expenditure is listed and assigned a dollar amount, and that an appropriate savings is set aside for irregular expenses and the emergencies that will happen.

- Tithe/Charitable Giving
- Savings
- Auto Insurance
- Auto Maintenance (oil change, tires, registration)
- Phone
- Laundry
- Toiletries
- Clothing
- Food (not in meal plan)
- Entertainment

I could list a lot of other things here, but you get the idea. It may take you three months to get this tweaked to your liking, but the key is to stick to it. There are plenty of budgeting apps for your phone. Many of you will use a debit card, but you might try using cash as well. Using cash gives you a greater appreciation for how much you're actually spending. At least with a debit card, you're only spending money you have. You've read this far and hopefully plan to put many of these concepts to work for you. Doing so, you'll avoid so much stress. Don't add the stress of debt.

Students have many opportunities to earn money or pay for things in addition to a traditional job. I'll give you a few examples. Departmental scholarships are easy to apply for during the semester and are set aside for students with solid GPAs. Imagine winning $500 each semester to cover all your books and fees. Every time you pay for goods or services, ask if there's a student discount. It's that simple, and it might shave fifty bucks a month from items on your budget. Dozens of people and organizations want to see you succeed and are happy to help financially. You're a student. Take the help and commit to help a student yourself one day.

Here's a final example that sums up this entire chapter. Does your degree offer a study abroad program over the summer or one semester? The cost alone might scare you. However, most of these also earn you credit that you would have spent on tuition. You might even ask some friends or family to match what you've saved toward your trip. Not only have you gathered funds for something exciting, but you've done it debt free. It might be something you can put on your resume, and it becomes a part of your degree that you've truly owned. That's working smarter, not harder.

Recommended Reading: Bissonnette, Zac. *Debt-Free U: How I Paid for an Outstanding College Education Without Loans, Scholarships, or Mooching off My Parents.* New York: Portfolio/Penguin, 2010.

14.

PREPARING TO LAUNCH

Throughout this book, I've told you to think like a professor, your roommate, someone in need, an opponent, and an employer. I'm going to add one more. Think like a professional. That's what you'll be once you graduate. A professional accountant, teacher, business manager, entrepreneur, engineer, historian, etc. Own it! You're putting a tremendous amount of time, money, and effort into your degree, all to set the stage for your professional life. But it starts today.

Admiral William McRaven gained some viral internet fame for a graduation speech he made where he encouraged graduates to begin their day by making their bed. Some scoffed, but they didn't really hear him. His point was that by making your bed you've started your day with an accomplishment and taken pride in yourself. This small success leads to another. One small thing leads to bigger things. Making the bed may not be the small act you do, but I hope you understand the importance of developing routines related to your professionalism.

These healthy habits begin now, continue through college, and weave throughout your life. Let's take the habit of budgeting as an example. Since you'll have had four years of budgeting experience, planning a post-college budget will only require adding or deleting some items and changing amounts. Budgeting is mostly about attitude and has little to do with math. My father always said, "You can live on whatever you make." Those that want to live above their means probably hate that statement, but he meant that most of us can certainly earn enough to plan a comfortable budget, with the right attitude.

You may not have noticed, but nearly every chapter dealt with relationships. Not just thinking like others but how you relate to others, how they help you, how you can help them, friendships, and working with your professor and other students (think co-workers). Relationships definitely come into play for those leaning toward a fraternity or sorority. Two things will have developed from all these relationships. First, you will have gained a ton of practical experience in dealing with people. Good and bad people. Easy and difficult people. The helpful and helpless. Those in authority over you and those you lead. You'll encounter these types for the rest of your life. Second, you may have met people you'll keep in touch with for the rest of your life. They might be friends or those you can network with during your career to help you get hired, make a sale, or coordinate in business.

Networking begins on day one, and you might consider challenging yourself with a networking goal. You could make this a point system with a goal of 100 points per semester. If you meet someone and exchange contact information, that's three points. If you meet for a meal and discuss your future, that's seven points. If you plan an event that you can list on your resume, that's fifteen points. You get the idea. A point system keeps you accountable and might make it fun.

While you should be thinking about your future career from day one, the school's network of connections and career center may be something that you spend more time on as you inch toward graduation. Your college will likely offer counselors to help you prepare resumes and connect with employers related to your degree field. They know which business owners are loyal to graduates from your school or who are partial to them because they know a particular department prepares graduates in the manner they see fit. That's a huge advantage you have over the generic applicant on the street.

Is graduate school next on your agenda after graduation? It probably doesn't need to be said, but if you've mastered the principles and tips I've discussed in this book, then you'll naturally use them in grad school and have a huge head start over those around you. These skills work in college and in life, so why wouldn't they work in grad school? Depending on your course of study, you might have fewer exams but a whole lot more reading and writing, but you're prepared for that. Attend every orientation session offered as they explain what to expect and what's expected of you. For example, during orientation law schools offer lectures on several study methods, such as group study, note-taking, class preparation, and how to read law textbooks. They'll add to the skills you've already learned.

Expect a different environment in graduate school, one that's more geared toward students working full-time who may be less interested in the school's social activities. That may be your mindset as well. Here's your opportunity to network with like-minded individuals that may very well be in your same industry. You may find someone with similar ambition as you that makes a great study or project partner.

I've emphasized relationships because you need to know that plenty of people want to see you succeed. Granted, you have to do the work, but you're not alone. Mastering college is not only about memory tips or using the math lab, but also about harnessing the wealth of help you have around you from technology and people.

We began by discussing grit and ended with making your bed. They both have so much to do with mastering college. They provide the determination to build habits for success. For working smarter not harder. That only slightly delay gratification. That free you from stress. That earn solid grades. That prepare you to master your career and life.

Recommended Reading: McRaven, William H. *Make Your Bed: Little Things That Can Change Your Life…and Maybe the World*. New York: Grand Central Publishing, 2017.

Acknowledgments

Thanks to my wife, Holly, and our five children, Kevin, Brandon, Jordan, Jadyn, and Megan, for their support and always cheering me on.

Thanks to the Rockwall Christian Writers Group for enduring first drafts and offering critiques.

Several beta readers reviewed the original manuscript and suggested improvements to deliver a better book for you than I could have done on my own. Thank you, Nick Woodall, Nancy Woodall, Brandon Sapp, Jordan Sapp, Jadyn Sapp, Susan Gordon, Paula Morgan, Ethan Nott, Nick Williamson, and Joseph Anway.

Thanks to my editor, Lauren Ruiz of Pure-Text.net, who does the real polishing. Thank you, Rebekah Haskell with vividcovers.com, who designed the cover.

Thank you, proofreaders: Mary Norsworthy, Debbie Vines, and Chris Tamez.

And a special thank you to those who asked me what I was working on, and when I answered, confirmed that this book is needed.

BIBLIOGRAPHY AND SUGGESTED RESOURCES

Adler, Mortimer J., and Van Doren Charles Lincoln. *How to Read a Book: The Classic Guide to Intelligent Reading*. New York: TouchStone, 2014.

Bissonnette, Zac. *Debt-Free U: How I Paid for an Outstanding College Education Without Loans, Scholarships, or Mooching off My Parents*. New York: Portfolio/Penguin, 2010.

Bluedorn, Nathaniel, Hans Bluedorn, Rob Corley, and Tim Hodge. *The Fallacy Detective: Thirty-Eight Lessons on How to Recognize Bad Reasoning*. Quartz Hill, CA: Christian Logic, 2015.

De Becker, Gavin. *The Gift of Fear*. London: Bloomsbury, 2000.

Duckworth, Angela. *Grit*. Toronto: Harper Collins Canada, 2018.

Gladwell, Malcolm. *Outliers: The Story of Success*. New York: Back Bay Books, Little, Brown and Company, 2013.

Lee, Harper. *To Kill a Mockingbird*. New York: Scribner Laidlaw, 1989.

McRaven, William H. *Make Your Bed: Little Things That Can Change Your Life…and Maybe the World*. New York: Grand Central Publishing, 2017.

Strunk, William, and E. B. White. *The Elements of Style*. New York: Macmillan, 1972.

I hope you enjoyed *Mastering College*. Would you mind posting a review and telling a friend about the book?

Join the mailing list at darrensapp.com for writing news and release dates of future books. You will not be spammed.

www.ingramcontent.com/pod-product-compliance
Lightning Source LLC
Chambersburg PA
CBHW070435010526
44118CB00014B/2051